Girls Know How®

Smart Alex

Written by
Ellen Langas Campbell

Ellen Langas

Cover Illustration by
April D'Angelo

A Kids Know How® Book

Kids Know How®

NouSoma Communications, Inc.

The rules in this fictional book are based on, but are not the actual rules of, the MATHCOUNTS® Competition Program. Please visit www.mathcounts.org to learn more about the Competition Program or the MATHCOUNTS Foundation.

First printing 2009

GIRLS KNOW HOW® and KIDS KNOW HOW® are registered trademarks of NouSoma Communications, Inc.

ISBN-13: 978-0-9743604-2-3
ISBN-10: 0-9743604-2-2

LCCN: 2008935704

ATTENTION SCHOOLS AND ORGANIZATIONS: Quantity discounts are available on bulk purchases of this book for educational or gift purchases. Special books or book excerpts also can be created to fit specific needs. For information, please contact NouSoma Communications, Inc., 35 Founders Way, Downingtown, PA 19335, 610-458-1580, books@nousoma.com.

Contents

Dedicated to my dear sister Rita L. Wilson
a talented teacher, coach and mother
and her daughter Alexandra

With special thanks to:
Dede Crough
Dr. Stephanie Pace Marshall, for sharing her story
MATHCOUNTS®

Much appreciation to:
Fabienne Anderson, Stephanie & Veronica Campbell
Kristen Chandler, Rebecca Divas
Brian Fillion, Angie Langas, Grace Lieblein
Dr. Pat McDonnell, Allison Morin
Randy Muller, Maggie Munts, Lee Nunnery
Emily Oulton, Lisa Populoh, Jen Rose
Katie & Karly Stec, Laurie Sutherland
Gesine Thomson and Cathy Tomlinson

1

"I'll collect the books, Mrs. Anderson!" Emily volunteered and shot to her feet to assist her teacher. *There she goes again with her perfect smile and perfect hair*, Alex thought. Emily dutifully picked up the books from each desk in Mrs. Anderson's 7th grade English class. The stack was reaching toward her chin and starting to slant slightly to the left.

As she approached, Alex's scowl turned into a devilish grin as she envisioned the perfect storm taking shape. A binder and three books lay under the desk in front of her, dangerously close to the aisle. Just an inch or two more and they would create a road block for unsuspecting Emily.

Alex slid forward in her chair, positioning her left foot just inches from the books. She focused, then stretched with all her might. *Contact.* Her foot nudged the binder, causing two books to slide directly into Emily's path.

Unaware of the hazard waiting inches away, Emily shuffled closer. Alex put on a winning smile and prepared to hand in her book. Emily's left foot landed squarely on one of the books in the aisle. The stack swayed in her arms. She lurched forward to balance the tower…three steps backward…two steps forward…but it was too late. Fourteen books toppled as she tried to grasp what was happening. Her face flushed while she grabbed at the air, desperately trying to catch the books as they tumbled to the floor like building blocks.

Some gasped, some giggled. Alex felt a secret rush of guilty pleasure as all eyes turned to her.

"Alex!" Mrs. Anderson's voice brought a sudden hush to the room.

"Yes, Mrs. Anderson?" Alex grinned innocently.

"You can add two more days of detention."

"Yes, Mrs. Anderson," Alex smoothly replied.

Detention had become routine for Alex this year; she had already racked up six days. It was an hour with Mrs. Marshall, one of the 7th grade math teachers. Alex simply doodled or closed her eyes. *Big deal.*

The bell rang and class was dismissed. Alex grabbed her backpack and a book from under her seat and left class with a slow, relaxed walk. She made deliberate eye contact with her teacher, but carefully displayed no emotion so all could witness her cool composure.

Once outside the door, she hurried directly to the girls' washroom. She slipped into one of the stalls and shut the door. Leaning with her back against the door, she waited for the thoughts in her head to stop racing. As she started to gather them, her eyes focused on the layers of graffiti that filled her small space. Meaningless phrases, pieces of bad poetry, doodles and other people's thoughts. She pulled out a marker and scrawled, *Does anyone know I'm here?*

"Hey, are you taking a bath in there?" Someone rapped on the door, and Alex realized she had better move along.

She came out and murmured "sorry" under her breath as her classmate nodded and said, "Good job! You made Emily look like an idiot. Way to go, Alex!"

"That's my job!" Alex called back. She caught herself in the mirror. *Nothing special,* she thought. Barely 5'3" at age 13, she examined her reflection. Thick, wavy brown hair framed her face. Not auburn, not chestnut, just brown. Today she wore it in a low ponytail. She probably should have washed it yesterday, but what was the point? Jeans, a t-shirt and sneakers without laces were her typical uniform. She pushed through the washroom door into the busy hallway and made her way to detention.

2

They sat next to each other in the front row, motionless. Four students sentenced to one hour of detention. All shared the common bond of boredom for the next sixty minutes.

Alex felt a pair of eyes on her and looked up to see Emily, who had just walked into the classroom with a few other students. Their eyes locked in awkward silence.

"What are you doing here?" Alex questioned forcefully. "You get a B or something?"

A boy snickered. Emily stiffened, but calmly stared back as she walked to the teacher's desk.

Alex got her pen out and started clicking it on and off on the top of her desk. It was a slow, methodical, *annoying* rhythm.

She noticed the clean smooth surface of her desk, like a canvas…so inviting. The doodles started with a few small circles in the corner, then she wrote, *Emily is in trouble.*

From the corner of her eye, Emily noticed the scribbling. She tried to ignore it, but couldn't.

"Stop it!"

"Stop what?"

"That!"

"You mean this?" Alex added *Big Trouble* to her work.

"That is so disrespectful."

"That is *so* disrespectful," Alex mocked.

Mrs. Marshall entered the room and Alex abruptly slid her pen into her pocket. For a woman in her mid-forties, Mrs. Marshall was fit, and Alex pondered whether she might have played sports when she was younger. She was a little taller than most of Alex's other female teachers, or maybe it was the way she carried herself that made her seem so. She had dark skin and wore her black hair pulled back tight in a low knot at the base of her neck. She was wearing a pale blue v-neck sweater over black pants and low black shoes. *Sensible shoes,* Alex thought. *Teacher shoes.* And she always wore the same pretty gold stud earrings. Her eyes were dark and piercing, and she was the kind of teacher who made you feel that she always knew what you were up to. Mrs. Marshall took note of the corner of Alex's desk, then greeted Emily and the students who had just walked in.

"I'll be right with you," she addressed the small group. She turned to Alex, and in the same pleasant tone continued, "Alex, I understand you will be joining us for another day, and I'm sure you can keep busy by washing the desktops in this room."

Alex responded with a blank stare.

"Good, then I see we understand each other," Mrs. Marshall confirmed.

Two more students came in to join Emily's group at the front of the room, and Mrs. Marshall welcomed them. Clearly, they were not there for detention.

"This is a nice turnout for our first MATHCOUNTS® meeting," Mrs. Marshall addressed the group. "The program is open to 6th, 7th and 8th graders, and I'm glad to see we have aspiring Mathletes® from each grade, including some from last year's team. We will be holding a competition in January to select a team of four students who will represent our school at the Chapter Competition in February. Winners will progress to the Illinois State Competition in March, and one team from our state will earn the right to advance to the MATHCOUNTS National Competition in May. Once our team is selected in January, we also will hold two practice competitions against schools in our county to help us prepare for the Chapter Competition. This includes competing against the East Middle School team that beat us last year, by four points I might add, and got to go to State Competition." Her announcement was met with eager smiles.

"I'm glad you are enthusiastic!" Mrs. Marshall added. "The purpose of our program is to get you excited about math and help you improve your math and analytical thinking skills, which will come in handy throughout your lives. Most importantly, we will have fun!"

Alex let out an audible groan. *Math fun? Now there's a contradiction in terms.* Other than passing her course, she saw no need for math in her future. It was a bore, and as far as she was concerned, the group of students assembled with Emily proved her point.

"This should be an exciting season," Mrs. Marshall continued. "From now through the first of the year, we will be practicing for our School Competition. We will meet here on Tuesday and Thursday afternoons after school until 4 o'clock to do a lot of warm-up problems. I will post a 'Problem of the Week' on the board each Tuesday and reveal the answer the following Tuesday.

"Our School Competition is in just seven weeks. So let's get started. Here are some practice problems." Mrs. Marshall passed out the problems and the students began their practice.

B-o-r-i-n-g, Alex thought. *Geeks and overachievers.* She put her head down and tried to doze. It seemed only minutes later it was time to go. She gathered her things and left the room, but not before rolling her eyes at Emily. When she opened the school's front double doors to step outside, a brisk breeze lifted her spirits. She turned on her iPod® and waved to her mom who was waiting for her in the parking lot. Her hair and make-up done to perfection, Mrs. Martinez pulled her BMW® to the curb to pick up Alex, who tossed her Dooney and Bourke® handbag in the backseat and climbed in the car next to her mother.

"Time to go home," her mother announced pleasantly.

"It's time to go home," she repeated.

"Alex!" She snapped awake at the sound of her name. Mrs. Marshall was standing over her desk.

"Perhaps if you spent your hour of detention more productively, there would be no need to nap. Why don't we start with cleaning up these desks on Tuesday? It's time to go home now."

"Yes, Mrs. Marshall," Alex responded, trying to regain her composure, while the other students fought to suppress giggles.

She grabbed her grey hooded sweatshirt and fumbled with her belongings as she attempted to leave the room quickly. This time when she pushed open the double doors, the picture was different. There was a chill in the air and dead leaves swirled around the sidewalk in her "windy city." She lived about twelve blocks from the school in Aurora, a town just outside Chicago, Illinois. The town was pretty and bustling. Office buildings, none higher than three or four stories, lined the streets, surrounded by retail stores and a few restaurants.

As she approached Minner Street, she quickened her pace. Her favorite store, Windy City Pets, was at the end of the street. A litter of kittens played in the front window. They were tiny, adorable fuzzy bundles. She stopped to admire the babies. Three slept in the corner in a pile of fluff…it was impossible to tell where one body ended and another began. Three other kittens were wide awake and scampering around their play area. Alex knelt on the sidewalk and pressed her face to the window to get as close as she could. She tapped gently on the window, attracting the attention of a tiger-striped kitten that inched nearer.

"Come on, little kitty," Alex coaxed as she tapped again.

Mr. Fillion, the store owner, appeared at the door and caught Alex's attention. An older man with white hair, bifocals and long gnarly fingers, he raised his eyebrow and sternly pointed to a sign, DO NOT TAP ON THE GLASS.

"Sorry, Miss Kitty," Alex whispered under her

breath. She glanced at Mr. Fillion as he wagged his finger at her, quickly gathered her things and left. Alex continued down the block watching her feet, squarely stepping on each crack in the sidewalk. Pretty homes with manicured lawns took the place of the office buildings for the next few blocks. At Shewmaker Street, the scenery abruptly changed.

The homes were still neatly maintained, but smaller, and some were in need of a fresh coat of paint. Most of the dwellings were duplexes, small buildings consisting of two homes side by side. Each had a porch with a rail dividing it from its neighbor. Just a block further was Alex's neighborhood. Some of her neighbors had recently lost their jobs. She saw them out in the brisk air, some chatting with each other, some sitting and thinking alone, perhaps trying to figure out how to make ends meet.

Alex's school day was in sharp contrast to the life she had at home. She arrived at her house and fished through her hoodie pockets for the door key. She found a note from her teacher that she was to get signed by her mother, letting her know about detention. *No rush for that* she thought, and crumpled it into the back pocket of her jeans. She located the key and proceeded to open the door. It creaked as it moved on its hinges, and once inside she had to use both hands and her shoulder to close it. The trick was to lift up on the knob with one hand while pushing hard with the other. Her mother had come up with this method and said there was no need to spend money fixing something if it wasn't necessary.

Dropping her backpack on the floor next to a little stand in the hallway, she kicked off her shoes and flicked on the light. Family pictures dotted the tabletops and walls. Handmade pillows and embroidered cloths brightened a small living area at the front of the house. Two worn armchairs and a loveseat surrounded a wooden coffee table. An arched doorway led to a clean but cluttered kitchen. A small table with three chairs surrounding it was pushed against the wall, and the stove, sink and refrigerator formed an L shape. Mrs. Martinez said if there was one thing she could have, it would be more drawer space and a dishwasher. Her two daughters were always quick to point out, "that's two things," and their mom would splash them with soap suds or wave the nearest utensil as she pretended to be mad. But she rarely got mad or complained, although she had a difficult life.

There was a back door to a yard that was about the size of an average one-car garage with a green wire fence around it. A staircase led from the living room up to Mrs. Martinez's room, a hall bathroom and the room Alex shared with her sister, Danielle. Alex headed up the twelve wooden steps covered with a worn blue carpet runner.

She entered her room and flopped on her bed. Her side of the room was dramatically different from Danielle's. Almost four years older, Danielle was much more interested in fashion, boys, music and make-up. She worked after school with her mother, but really wanted to be a hair stylist. Alex had to admit her sister was talented. Her girlfriends would stop over and Danielle would play with their hair, experimenting with buns, braids and up-dos, usually resulting in fantastic styles, although once in a while, a disaster! Danielle always wanted to get her hands on her sister's long locks, but Alex was quick to avoid her.

Alex's side of the room was decorated with posters of places to which she hoped to travel. New York City and Los Angeles topped her list. Her mother reminded her that the wonderful city of Chicago was only a train ride away, but Alex insisted that New York and Los Angeles were the ultimate! A poster of the New York City skyline filled her wall. She displayed a snow globe with the Empire State Building in it and a postcard that featured the famous HOLLYWOOD sign in California on her desk, next to a photo of her mother and father.

Alex's parents grew up in the same section of Chicago, where Spanish was the main language. Her mother didn't learn to speak English well until she was in school. At 15 she dropped out of high school to get a job cleaning offices and help raise her four younger siblings. When she was 18, she met Alex's dad, and they married a year later. After Alex was born, they moved to their current home. Both were hard workers, proud of their rich Hispanic heritage, and often spoke Spanish at home when they conversed with each other. They hoped to make a better life for their family.

Mr. Martinez was born in Cuba and fled to the United States with his family when he was just four years old. He was a happy, ambitious man who worked in a shoe store, but always said that one day he and Mrs. Martinez would realize their dream of opening a restaurant together. He was a superb cook, and although money was tight, Sunday dinner was always a special treat. On Sunday afternoons, he and Alex would walk to the market and pick out fresh ingredients, then return and fill the house with wonderful aromas that made her mouth water. He loved to play games, and after dinner he would present the girls with a riddle or brain teaser. Alex loved this time they spent together, and especially enjoyed it when she would beat her sister to the answer! Mr. Martinez always had a little piece of candy hidden in his pocket as a reward.

When Alex turned eight, the shoe store closed and Mr. Martinez was out of a job. Soon after, he became ill and died within a year, leaving Mrs. Martinez, Danielle and Alex on their own.

It was hard to believe nearly five years had passed. When Danielle turned 15, she joined their mother cleaning offices after school. Sometimes they didn't get home till eight o'clock. Alex figured that when she turned 15 she would help her mom as well. That's what all the women in her family had done for generations.

Her mother and sister had already left for the evening. Alex would do her homework, heat up a plate of food her mom left in the refrigerator for dinner and read or watch some TV until their return. That's the way pretty much every Monday through Thursday evening went. She stared at her poster of New York for a moment longer, then went downstairs to get her homework started.

3

It was Tuesday morning and Alex did her best to ignore Emily in homeroom. Chimes signaled the start of the school day. *Ding, dong, ding…*it sounded like someone was hitting three notes on a xylophone in thirds, but it was actually a pre-recorded tape. Then the principal, Ms. Crowell, read the announcements.

> *Good morning. Attention all sixth grade students, tomorrow is the class field trip to Fermilab in Batavia. Please remember to bring a lunch, and if you have not turned in your permission slip, you must bring it with you tomorrow or you will not be able to go. Money for the giftwrap fundraiser is due next Tuesday. We are pleased to announce that once again West Middle School will enter a team into the MATHCOUNTS competition. This will be our second year, and we have high hopes to send a team to the State Competition. Last year we performed very well in our Chapter Competition, placing second after East. We will hold a School Competition immediately after holiday break to help select*

our team. Any student who is interested in participating can sign up in Mrs. Marshall's classroom. Practices will be held Tuesday and Thursday afternoons in her room from three o'clock till four o'clock. Don't miss out on this chance to have fun and learn skills that you can use the rest of your life!

Oh brother, the Mathletes are at it again, Alex thought and glanced at Emily. *She must be in heaven.*

~ ~ ~

At lunch, Alex sat with her regular group. It wasn't really "her" group, it was just "a" group. Everyone seemed to fit into a clique or group, but she never felt she quite fit with any of them. They all had labels...the *popular* girls, the *mean* girls, the *brainiacs*, the *jocks*, the *geeks*. If her table had a label, it probably would have been the *misfits*. The six boys and girls who sat together marched to their own beats. Maybe that's why she felt comfortable with them. They sat at the opposite end of the table from the mean girls, so it was a pretty sure thing that no one from another table would bother them.

Alex usually sat next to MaryBeth, who always dressed in black and wore heavy eyeliner to match. She was a pretty girl, but the make-up

16

made her appear angry. No one spoke to her, but Alex would chat with her every so often, and discovered she was actually very nice. Then there was Ben, who was in her English class and into playing the saxophone. His grades suffered, but he was a fantastic musician. He really didn't care one way or another with whom he ate lunch. Matt was a star on the baseball team in seventh grade last year, but after getting hurt in a car accident, he had to stop playing. He had been considered one of the jocks, but now he wasn't really part of that group anymore. He felt a little lost without his old label. Kit was new to the school and just showed up at the table one day and had been sitting there ever since. She also was in Alex's homeroom. She talked non-stop, even when no one was listening. Brian was the oldest at the table. He had been held back a year and had been in and out of trouble all through middle school. Others would come and go, but that was the usual crew.

"What is this?" Matt displayed a deep fried oval-shaped piece of food on his fork.

"Chicken," MaryBeth murmured without looking up.

"How do you know it's chicken? It could be anything."

"It's chicken."

"It could be fish, or pork, or a potato."

"It's chicken."

"But how d'ya know?"

"'Cause it says chicken on the menu on the chalkboard, actually," Kit pointed out with authority.

"It doesn't look like chicken."

Ben wadded up his napkin and flicked it at Matt, hitting him squarely in the forehead.

"Ouch, fine, it's chicken," Matt gave in.

"Anyone going to the Bears game on Sunday?" Matt posed the question to the table, but no one responded.

"Yeah, my dad's going to try to get tickets to a game this year," he continued.

Alex pulled an apple out of her lunch bag and took a loud bite that underscored the silence at the table.

"Yeah, that would be cool," Matt continued.

"I guess those who can't play sports, just watch them," Brian announced casually.

Matt ruffled at the remark.

"That wasn't very nice," Kit defended Matt.

"I'm just saying," Brian responded while checking to see if there was anything left in his bag.

"I'll play ball again," Matt said.

"Sure you will."

"I will."

"Maybe you should try being a *Mathlete* since you sure aren't going to be an *ath-a-lete*," Brian dragged out the syllables.

"You don't know anything," Matt blurted out. "I'll play ball again. What do you know anyway? You couldn't add your way out of a box!"

The comment caught everyone's attention. MaryBeth stifled a giggle, Ben came right out and laughed, and Matt quickly examined his sandwich, realizing that he made no sense at all.

The bell rang, not a minute too soon for Matt. Alex made her way to her next class. Just three more periods and the day was over. Except for detention.

4

Alex shuffled to Mrs. Marshall's classroom.

"Good afternoon, Alex," Mrs. Marshall said as Alex entered the room. She nodded toward the board. Alex looked at it, but it was blank. Then she saw a bucket of water, a spray bottle and a sponge on the floor right below the board and realized what Mrs. Marshall had in mind. "I thought you would want to get started cleaning desktops this afternoon."

"Right." Alex sauntered toward the supplies, picked them up and arranged them at her desk.

The other students started filing into the room...those for detention, and those who hoped to be on the MATHCOUNTS team. *Could there be two more opposite groups?* Alex wondered.

When Emily walked in, the boys sitting next to Alex stopped talking and looked up. Emily glanced at them, but didn't acknowledge them.

"Hi, Mrs. Marshall," her voice sounded like honey.

"Good afternoon, Emily," Mrs. Marshall replied. "All set for practice?"

"Sure, I can't wait for our first Problem of the Week!"

How could she get so excited over a math problem? Alex groaned. *What was it about Emily that made everyone take notice anyway? Sure, she was a little taller, and maybe a little more slender. She took the time to fix her strawberry blonde hair...but that headband...ick. And her outfit...way too preppy. What's with the popped collar? Was it possible for someone to be too neat? That's it! She's just too neat. It's the end of the day, and she is still neat. That's just one more thing not to like about her.*

Emily must have felt Alex's gaze and glanced at her. Alex made a face and Emily responded with a look of indifference, then took note of the cleaning supplies and smiled.

"Her mother is a cleaning lady, too," Emily whispered to the others, making sure Alex heard. Alex tried to hide the sting of embarrassment and quickly turned away.

Mrs. Marshall gathered the group together and started doing Warm-Up exercises - questions from the MATHCOUNTS School Handbook that students had to figure out without calculators.

Judy buys hot dogs that come in packages of six, and she buys hot dog buns that come in packages of eight. What is the minimum number of hot dog packages she can buy in order to be able to buy an equal number of hot dogs and hot dog buns?

21

The Mathletes quickly picked up their pencils and scratched away on their papers. "If you have the answer, place your pencil down and raise your hand," Mrs. Marshall instructed.

I have the answer, Alex thought. *The answer is zero. Because Judy doesn't like hot dogs, she decides to get burgers. Ha!*

Emily slammed down her pencil and shot her hand into the air.

"Emily," Mrs. Marshall called on her.

"The answer is 4 packages. Judy can buy 4 packages of hot dogs which is equivalent to 24 hot dogs. Then she can buy 3 packages of buns to also equal 24."

"Very good, Emily."

"Very good, Emily," Alex muttered under her breath.

"Alex, do you have something to say?" Mrs. Marshall turned her attention to Alex.

"Uh, no," she murmured.

Mrs. Marshall raised her eyebrow and turned her attention back to her group. "Let's try another one."

Jerry has a jar that contains only nickels, dimes and quarters. There is at least one of each type of coin in the jar. If the total value of the coins in the jar equals 60 cents, how many quarters are in the jar?

The Mathletes scrambled to solve the problem.

Once again Emily's hand flew into the air as she dramatically slammed her pencil on her desktop.

"Emily?" Mrs. Marshall nodded.

"Emily?" Alex murmured in a mocking tone.

"Alex!" Mrs. Marshall snapped.

Alex squirmed as all eyes turned to her.

"Is there something you would like to say?"

"No, ma'am."

"Maybe if you spent more time working instead of talking, you could be part of a select group like this."

"Yes, ma'am."

"Then maybe you would be able to solve a problem like this, too."

"Yes, ma'am."

"I don't expect any more outbursts from you unless you plan to answer one of the questions."

"Like that's going to happen," one of the Mathletes chimed in.

One of the girls just shook her head at Alex, and Emily smirked. Mrs. Marshall turned her attention back to her group.

"One," Alex murmured.

Mrs. Marshall turned to Alex and asked sharply, "Did you say something?"

"One."

"One what?"

"One quarter."

"Oh," Mrs. Marshall looked into her answer book and paused. "Why, yes, that is correct." There was an awkward silence in the room. "But next time, please raise your hand if you are going to participate."

"Yes, ma'am."

5

A week later Alex sat, or more accurately slumped, in her chair during English class. The students were taking turns reading book reports. The sound of a steady low voice lulled Alex into relaxation. Her head nodded forward and her eyelids flickered as she struggled to stay awake.

"Alex?" Mrs. Anderson's voice cracked. She opened her eyes and was struck with the sting of fluorescent lighting. All eyes were on her. "We're waiting for your answer."

"Could you repeat the question, please?"

"No, but I will give you a new question," Mrs. Anderson replied. "Would you like to add a day of after-school detention to your current six days?"

Whatever, Alex thought and then said, "Yes, Mrs. Anderson."

"If I didn't know better, I would guess you liked detention, Miss Martinez," her teacher scolded.

~ ~ ~

The Problem of the Week was on the board when Alex arrived at Mrs. Marshall's room:

For the arithmetic sequence 1000, 987, 974, 961...what is the least positive integer in the sequence?

Oh joy. Detention. Alex rambled over to her seat to watch the Mathletes in action. The typical group of team wannabes came in and took their spots. Then Matt walked in. *Detention is looking up,* Alex thought. She would have a partner in crime. Matt saw Alex and their eyes locked. He looked like a deer caught in headlights. Instead of walking over to sit at the empty desk next to her, he joined the group with Mrs. Marshall. Alex's jaw dropped. *Traitor! Could he be serious? Matt... a Mathlete? What was the world coming to?*

The students did their traditional "Warm-Ups" and "Workouts" and finished up in about an hour. As soon as the group broke up, Matt left quickly, without acknowledging Alex. Mrs. Marshall dismissed her, and she raced after him.

"Matt!" she called out after him, but he pretended not to hear.

"Matt! I know you can hear me."

He stopped and waited.

"What were you thinking?" Alex demanded.

Matt's face flushed. "I dunno."

"That's for sure!"

"It's just that since I can't play baseball, I want to do something important. I know that no one thinks I have a brain, but I think I can do this."

"Matt! You are hanging around with a bunch of nerds who think calculators are fashion accessories."

"It's not like that, Alex. They're okay. In fact they really accept me. And they're smart." He hesitated and added, "And fun and kinda nice."

"Oh please," Alex sighed with exaggeration.

"Look, Alex, I'd really appreciate it if you didn't bring this up at lunch, okay?"

"I gotta go," Alex replied. She turned in the opposite direction and walked away.

~ ~ ~

All the way home, Alex fumed, thinking about how Matt had betrayed their group.

She took solace in watching the kittens play in the window of the pet store. *Fun and nice? Was he kidding? Does he think Emily is nice? And fun?* She didn't see any sign of Mr. Fillion, so she squatted down in front of the window and admired "her" kittens. Miss Kitty was there along with her brothers and sisters. Pretty soon they would be old enough for lucky families to take them home.

"I won't let anyone take you, Miss Kitty," Alex whispered to the window.

"Ahem." Mr. Fillion startled her. He was standing in the doorway with his hands on his hips. Alex startled, jumped up and ran. Mr. Fillion chuckled to himself and went back inside his shop.

6

That evening, Mrs. Martinez and Danielle returned home early from work, so the three could enjoy dinner together. Mrs. Martinez seemed upset. She unfolded a wrinkled piece of paper at the table.

"I found a note from your English teacher in your jeans when I was doing the laundry," she said to Alex. "It says that you have been interrupting class and staying after school in detention. Is this true, Alex?"

Alex felt her throat tighten up. Danielle looked at her with an annoyed expression.

"It's kinda true."

"How do you mean?" her mother asked.

"Well, she just doesn't like me."

"She writes that you disrupt the class. This is very embarrassing to me. It's not the way I raised you. You did not tell me this has been happening."

"I know," Alex said quietly, lowering her eyes.

"You better shape up, kid," Danielle added.

"What do you know?" Alex snapped.

"All I know is that I work hard all day at school, then come home and work hard with Mom."

"Yeah, you work hard cleaning houses and offices. So what's the point of school anyway? Since when did you want to be a cleaning lady? I thought you wanted to go to beauty school. You are going to turn out just like Mom. Is that what you want for me, too?"

Danielle gasped and Mrs. Martinez looked at Alex in stunned silence.

"Is this what you think of your mother?" Mrs. Martinez asked, her voice shaking. "Do you think this is the life I wished for myself and you girls? I have a job that I do with pride, and it pays enough money for us to have a home and food on the table." Her eyes filled with tears and she left the room.

"You're an idiot," Danielle barked as she left to check on her mother.

Alex sat alone at the table. *I am an idiot. How could I be so cruel to Mom? There is just so much I want that I'll never have. But I guess some people aren't so lucky.* She cleared the dishes from the table and washed them, dried her hands and went up to her room.

7

There was tension in the air at the lunch table the next day. Alex was quiet and Matt wouldn't make eye contact with anyone.

"What's the matter, everyone?" Kit asked cheerfully. "Only ten days until winter vacation! We should be happy!"

No one responded. Matt sat in fear that Alex would tell his secret. Alex grabbed her lunch bag, walked out of the cafeteria and headed for the library. She didn't feel like talking to anyone. She sat at an empty table and pulled out a book but wasn't really reading. About ten minutes had passed when she heard someone groan, followed by a "darn." She looked behind her to discover Emily working on the Problem of the Week.

Pitiful, Alex thought. Emily's head was always buried in a book, or she was running off to take piano, dance or singing lessons. It seemed like her life revolved around being good at everything. Alex wondered how she had the time to do it all. Emily lived in the part of town that everyone envied, complete with big houses, big cars and big yards. But for someone who had everything, she sure didn't seem very happy about it.

Emily could feel someone looking at her and spun around.

"Hi," Alex said, catching Emily by surprise.

"Hi," she replied cautiously as she wondered what nasty trick Alex had up her sleeve.

"Having trouble with the Problem of the Week?"

"A little," Emily said, trying not to admit confusion. Then she followed up with a firm, "Yes."

"It's a tough one," Alex said as she gathered her things to go.

"It is," Emily replied, still suspicious.

"Try twelve."

"Twelve?" Emily repeated.

"Yeah, twelve."

8

The following Tuesday after school, with the exception of Alex who sat glumly in detention, all eyes were on Mrs. Marshall when she announced, "Let's start with the Problem of the Week." No one raised his or her hand.

"Anyone?" Mrs. Marshall asked. "I was hoping someone took a stab at it, but it looks like no one did."

Emily cleared her throat and raised her hand halfway into the air.

"Emily?" Mrs. Marshall called on her.

"I worked on the problem," she announced.

"Good, and what answer did you get?"

Emily paused, then glanced at Alex. Alex watched with a blank expression.

Mrs. Marshall noticed the exchange and asked again, "Your answer is?"

"Twelve."

"Very good, Emily. Twelve is correct."

There was a small round of applause. *Oh brother, I think I'm going to be ill,* Alex thought.

Mrs. Marshall looked at Alex, then back at Emily, asking her, "And how did you arrive at twelve?"

"Um, what do you mean, Mrs. Marshall?" she asked.

"I mean, how did you work out the problem to come up with that answer?"

"Well, let me think," Emily stalled. She could feel her heart beat faster and her thoughts started spinning, making it hard to concentrate. She looked at her paper. It had no work on it at all. Her face became flushed. The sound of a textbook hitting the floor interrupted the awkward moment. All eyes turned to Alex, who shrugged her shoulders and picked up the book that had fallen from her desk. Emily quickly looked down again and twirled her hair, then continued, "It's funny, I must have forgotten my notes in my locker."

"Very well. Let's move on, then. We have one more day of practice until our holiday break. When we return, anyone who wishes to enter the School Competition may do so the first week of January, right here in my classroom. The four students who have the highest scores will be our MATHCOUNTS team for two practice competitions in January and the actual Chapter Competition in February." Alex and the other students in detention pretended to show excitement, grasping their faces with two hands in mock surprise, much as a pageant winner might do. Mrs. Marshall added, "And since my students who are here for detention seem so interested, they can join us for the test, too."

Oh, that's just great, Alex thought. The Mathletes worked on their problems and Alex doodled until practice was over and the students were dismissed.

After saying goodbye to the students, Mrs. Marshall picked up her phone and dialed Mrs. Anderson's extension.

"Hello?" Mrs. Anderson's voice came through the speakerphone.

"It's Donna. Our little project is in the works, and she is on her way," Mrs. Marshall alerted her with her best attempt at sounding like an undercover agent.

"Roger that!" Mrs. Anderson replied with a smile in her voice.

A moment later, Alex passed Mrs. Anderson's room.

"Alex!" Mrs. Anderson called out. Alex backed up a few feet to see the teacher at her desk. "I heard from your mother. I understand you had not told her you were going to after-school detention. Can you tell me why?"

Alex pondered the question, but couldn't think of a good answer. "No, I guess I really don't know why."

"You don't seem very interested in class," Mrs. Anderson continued. "You seem like a bright girl, but you don't hand in a number of assignments. Is there a reason for that?"

"I don't know."

"Don't you think English is important?"

"I guess so."

"What do you mean by that?"

"I don't know." Alex dropped her head and remained quiet. Mrs. Anderson waited patiently for her to speak again.

"I guess I really don't see how anything you are teaching has anything to do with me. I mean, why do I need to know English or history or math if I'm going to be cleaning houses when I get out of school?"

"Is that what you expect to do?"

"I guess so. Seems like that's what all the women in my family do."

"Do you want to talk about it?"

"No, I gotta go." She turned to head to the door.

Mrs. Anderson's brow furrowed in frustration as she watched Alex leave.

"Not so fast, Miss Martinez," she quickly called out.

Alex stopped and turned toward her.

"I'll let Mrs. Marshall know to expect you the

first afternoon back from holiday break."

"Oh, right," Alex said without showing any emotion. "Thank you," Alex said insincerely as she left.

Mrs. Anderson sat motionless for a short time, watching the empty space where Alex had stood. A smile slowly formed on her face. She picked up the classroom phone and dialed Mrs. Marshall's extension. "Hello, Donna. All systems go for Project Smart Alex!"

9

Later that evening, Alex was reading her library book on the steps when Danielle arrived home from work. Danielle stood just two inches taller than Alex and had a stronger build. Her dark wavy hair was thick and lush, and she wore it pulled back in a tight ponytail. A thin line of dark blue eyeliner surrounded her brown eyes. She wore a long-sleeved t-shirt and jeans with sneakers. As she approached, she undid the band, allowing her hair to fall loosely around her shoulders.

"Outta the way, kid!" Danielle ordered as she made her way up the steps to their room. Alex didn't budge and went back to reading.

"Move it."

"You move it."

Danielle made her way around Alex and climbed two more steps, then paused. "You shouldn't have lied to Mom," she scolded.

"It wasn't a lie," Alex defended herself. "I just didn't tell her everything."

"Same thing," Danielle concluded.

"Whatever."

"You should have told Mom you had detention."

"I know," Alex admitted. "And to make matters worse, Mrs. Anderson just slammed me with more when we get back from break."

"What did you get detention for anyway?"

"I dunno," Alex shrugged.

"I'm sure you have an idea," Danielle said sarcastically. "You've been there almost every week."

"I guess I forget to turn in my homework sometimes."

"I find that a little hard to believe. You do your homework every night. If I didn't know better, I'd think you wanted to stay after school."

"It would be better than coming home and cleaning houses."

"Hey, that's my job you're talking about."

"Exactly," Alex emphasized the point. "Why is that your job? It sure isn't the job you want."

"It's a good job and Mom needs help."

"What happened to your dream of working in a salon?"

"It's just a silly dream."

"Well, it's not going to happen cleaning houses."

"That's just the way it is around here, Alex. Don't you get it? Have you looked around lately? Has anyone ever left the neighborhood?"

Alex stared back in silence.

"Have they?" Danielle demanded.

"No."

"So what makes you think you're any different from me and everyone else?"

Alex could feel her eyes starting to well with tears and turned her face away from her sister.

"Maybe that's not what I want. And maybe I'd rather stay at school than come home so I can become a cleaning person."

"Are you kidding me? You stay after school on purpose?"

"I dunno. Maybe."

"You're crazy."

"Who's the crazy one? Take a look in the mirror. You want to be a hair stylist. You're really good, and you do nothing to make it happen."

Alex got up from the steps and went to their room. She stood staring at her poster of New York City, pulled out the tacks that held it in place, rolled it up and stuffed it under her bed.

10

The holidays blew in with a cold blast of arctic air. The winter break was a welcome change of pace at the Martinez home. Mrs. Martinez had time off from work, so she and the girls baked cookies, shopped for gifts and prepared a holiday feast together. It seemed that the festive days had passed too quickly when it was time to return to the routine of school.

~ ~ ~

The first afternoon after holiday break was a Thursday, and Mrs. Marshall's room was overflowing with students and chatter after school. About forty kids had shown up to the School Competition to land a spot on the MATHCOUNTS team. It took a while for Mrs. Marshall to get the students' attention so she could pass out the competitions. Matt sat in front of Alex and passed a booklet to her, who in turn passed a booklet to the student behind her. Emily was sitting to her right and flashed Alex a fake smile. Mrs. Marshall gave directions, set a timer for forty minutes and announced, "Begin!"

About ten minutes into the competition, one student noisily gathered her belongings, dropped her booklet into the trash and left. Emily whispered to Alex, "It's not too late to run away, Alex."

"I'm not even trying out for your stupid team," Alex whispered back. "Mrs. Marshall is making me take the competition. It's like punishment."

"Quiet, please," Mrs. Marshall silenced the girls.

About twenty minutes later, Alex put down her pencil and slid her booklet out of the way. She leaned back, stretched her legs out and closed her eyes.

When Mrs. Marshall glanced up to check on the group, she noticed Alex dozing and walked over to her.

"Alex," she addressed her in a low voice.

Alex opened her eyes, but did not sit up.

"I thought you understood that you would be taking the competition along with the other students."

A reprimand, Emily thought as she looked on with pleasure.

"I did, I'm done."

"Fine. But I would have appreciated it if you took this more seriously. You may wait here, awake, until time is up and everyone is dismissed."

"Got it," Alex nodded and slid lower in her chair. She could hear others whispering and knew they were talking about her. *Fine.*

"Time," Mrs. Marshall announced calmly about ten minutes later. "Please put your pencils down. Place your booklets on my desk on your way out. We will announce results Monday morning. The top four students will be placed on our competition team. We will hold two practice competitions against schools from our county in two weeks so we can sharpen our skills for the Chapter Competition in February. The rest of you may all continue to attend practices on Tuesdays and Thursdays. Thank you for participating."

One by one, students dropped their booklets on Mrs. Marshall's desk and filed out of the room. Emily kissed her booklet ceremoniously for luck and placed it neatly on top of the pile. Alex placed hers on the opposite side of the desk, by itself, as a deliberate reminder that she had no intention of trying out for the team.

As soon as the students hit the hallway, the chatter broke out.

"What did you get for number six?" a student questioned the group.

"I got 81," another replied. "What did you get?"

"You're wrong," Emily flatly announced to the group. "I got 9. You had to take the square root."

"Oh no!"

"Oh well, better luck next time," she said smugly.

~ ~ ~

That evening, Mrs. Martinez and Danielle got home around 7:30, and Danielle went straight up to the bedroom, turned on her CD player and picked up a magazine. Alex was reading on her bed and mumbled, "Turn it down." Danielle ignored her sister. Alex rolled out of her bed, walked over to the player, turned down the volume and situated herself back on her bed.

"Don't touch my stuff," Danielle commanded.

"Creep."

"Brat," Danielle retorted.

"Girls!" Mrs. Martinez called up the steps.

"Sorry."

"Sorry."

Alex saw that Danielle was reading a fat magazine. "Whatcha reading?"

"It's really cool," Danielle said as she showed her sister the cover. "I was cleaning at Bella Salon today, and they let me take it. I can keep it! There are hundreds of fantastic hair styles in it. Look!"

Alex flopped on the bed next to her sister and they turned the pages together, commenting on the styles.

"Pretty!"

"Yeah, I like it, too," Danielle agreed and

flipped to another page.

"Oh my gosh…it looks like she stuck her finger into an electrical socket!" she laughed, pointing to another style.

"Ha! It does. How about this one? It would be so pretty for a wedding…or the prom," Alex continued.

"Want to try it?"

"What, on me?"

"Yes, on you."

Alex slid off the bed and looked in the mirror. She pictured herself with a pretty hairstyle and an outfit to match. Winding her hair up on top of her head and walking like a model, she mugged for her sister and they both giggled. Looking at her reflection, she let her hair drop around her shoulders, sighed and said, "Thanks anyway." She plopped back onto her bed and said, "I think I'll get to bed early tonight."

Danielle shrugged her shoulders and continued browsing through her magazine.

11

Monday morning at school, the halls were buzzing with conversation. Alex stopped at her locker and hung her coat, then sauntered into Mrs. Anderson's homeroom.

"What's the big deal?" she asked Kit.

"They announce the MATHCOUNTS team this morning," Kit said, as if everyone should have known.

*Ding, dong, ding...*the morning announcements began.

> *Good morning, boys and girls.*
> *Physicals for spring sports are scheduled today after school. Make sure to bring signed forms for boys and girls track, baseball and boys tennis.*
> *Congratulations to the members of this year's MATHCOUNTS team who will represent our school during our upcoming county practice rounds and Chapter Competition in February. Your new members are:*
> *Emily Crough*
> *David Liu*

Janella Ritter
and Matt Bauer.

What? Alex wondered if she heard correctly. Could Matt really be on the competition team? Was the whole world going crazy?

~ ~ ~

Later that day, Matt braced himself as he approached the lunch table. A knot had formed in his stomach. He had considered going to the nurse's office to beg her to send him home for the afternoon. Anything would be better than enduring the lunch group today. When he reached the table, everyone was already there. Hoping not to attract attention, he quietly sat down and took a peanut butter and jelly sandwich out of his bag. *Maybe it will be alright after all,* he determined and started to relax.

Brian took a bag of M&Ms® from his lunch, and a wicked smile stretched across his face. He caught Ben's eye as he ripped open the bag and ceremoniously placed the candies on his napkin one at a time.

"Gee," he announced, attracting the attention of everyone at the table, as well as some who surrounded their group. "If Susie had six green pieces of candy, four yellow and three red…how many pieces of candy would she have?"

46

Ben responded in pretend confusion, "Gee, I don't know."

"Do you know, MaryBeth?"

"I have no idea," MaryBeth shrugged her shoulders.

"I bet I know who would know," Brian said slowly as he turned his head to Matt. All eyes at the table were now transfixed on him. "Matt the Mathlete!"

Matt flushed. Suddenly he couldn't swallow the bite of sandwich that was in his mouth. The peanut butter felt like glue.

Ben continued without missing a beat, "If Brian had 12 marbles and gave MaryBeth four and me three, how many marbles would he have left? Matt, do you know how many marbles are left?"

Matt could hear the kids talking, feel their gaze, but simply couldn't respond. It was as if he was frozen in time.

Alex crumpled her lunch bag, diverting the attention away from Matt. She got up and nodded to Matt to do the same. "I know the answer," she announced. "Brian has nothing left, because everyone lost their marbles."

Kit laughed out loud at Alex's remark and then quieted herself when Ben shot her a disapproving look. Matt and Alex left the table. Brian looked around as everyone waited in uncomfortable silence to hear what he would say in response. But he said nothing. He fumbled with his candy, picked up a red piece and tossed it above his head, catching it in his mouth.

Matt and Alex walked into the hallway in silence. "Thanks, Alex," Matt said.

"You weren't exactly on a roll in there," Alex replied.

"I didn't know what to say. I'm not even sure what I want. I mean, I think it's great to be on the math team, but…"

"You'd rather be playing ball," Alex finished his sentence.

"Yeah."

"I think whatever you choose, as long as it's what you want to be doing, it's fine. If you want to be a Mathlete, then do it. Look how many people tried out, and you got on the team. And I think you'll play baseball again, heck, you've been walking so well, you'd never even know you broke your leg."

"Really, do you think so? Thanks! I mean, I have been working out really hard and I feel better than ever, and the sports physicals are this afternoon. Who knows, maybe I'll get cleared to play again."

"That's the spirit. Anything can happen. You

just have to be ready to take advantage of the opportunity. You are lucky, you actually have choices. Not everyone does. You have to make up your mind, and then go after it. It doesn't matter what everyone else thinks."

"Gee, Alex. You're not as mean as I thought you were."

Alex made a pretend frown.

"I mean that it a nice way. You know what I mean."

"Yeah, I know what you mean."

Alex headed off to English class as her thoughts wandered. *I wish I knew what I wanted to do...*

Mrs. Anderson had an assignment on the board when the students arrived – *Women of Achievement.*

"Good afternoon, class," she said as the students settled into their seats. "Today and tomorrow you are going to research and give presentations about women of achievement."

"This should be a short class," one of the boys yelled out.

"That will be quite enough," Mrs. Anderson reprimanded. "I'd like each of you to select a woman who has succeeded in her chosen field and prepare a two-page report. This can be someone in business or science, sports, charitable work...or in just about any area. The important thing is to discover and write about what helped her become a success, what motivated her, how did she get to the top of her field? Did she face any challenges? Learn about her background and upbringing, think about what makes her different than you and what makes her similar."

"I can think of one thing that's different," Ben blurted out. "She wears dresses and I don't." Laughter broke out in the classroom.

"Thank you very much, Ben," Mrs. Anderson smiled as she continued, "I think everyone understands the assignment. I've borrowed a number of books from the library that you may utilize, and you can also use our classroom computers to do some research on the Internet. I've posted a list on the back bulletin board that might give you some ideas. You have the rest of the period to select someone to profile and get started."

The students went about their research while Mrs. Anderson walked around the room, stopping to offer help where needed. She spotted Alex writing intently in her notebook.

"It looks like you are off and running on this project," she said with approval. As she glanced at the notebook, Mrs. Anderson realized the work was an elaborate doodle of the letters "NYC." "Perhaps you could spend the same effort picking a research topic," she suggested. "Having trouble finding someone to profile?"

"No." Alex paused. "Maybe."

"What seems to be the problem?"

"I don't know," Alex mumbled. "It just seems that half of the women I read about had it made by the time they were born. They did everything right. They went to the best schools, knew all the right people. It sure would be nice to see someone like, someone like, I dunno..."

"Someone like, you?" Mrs. Anderson suggested.

"Well, maybe, yeah."

"Hmm," Mrs. Anderson considered. "Interesting point. Keep working on it, and in the meantime, maybe this will be of interest." Mrs. Anderson placed a photocopied article on Alex's desk and walked to the other side of the room to help another student. Alex pushed the paper around for a little bit, started folding it into a paper airplane and finally read it. About five minutes later she walked over to the row of computers.

"Hey, can I use the computer when you're finished?" she asked.

"Sure, you can have it now," her classmate replied. Alex worked until the bell rang.

On her way out, Alex passed by Mrs. Anderson's

desk and asked, "Did you plan to give that article to me?"

"Let's just say I had a hunch you might like it."

Alex nodded and left the room without responding.

Less than a minute passed when Alex walked back in.

"Yes, Alex?" Mrs. Anderson acknowledged her.

"Thanks," Alex murmured, and left.

Mrs. Anderson smiled in return, cleaned up her desk, turned off the light and closed the door behind her. A few minutes later, the halls had cleared and the sound of her heels echoing in the quiet hallways made her feel self-conscious. She slowed as she approached Mrs. Marshall's room and ducked her head in the doorway to see Matt Bauer just leaving.

"Thank you, Mrs. Marshall," he said politely as he left her room. He nodded to Mrs. Anderson as he passed her in the doorway.

"Hello, Matt," Mrs. Anderson said and nodded in return.

"And good afternoon to you," Mrs. Anderson continued cheerily to Mrs. Marshall.

Mrs. Marshall was cleaning up her room, preparing to leave for the day.

"Hi!"

"So what do you think of our little plan?" Mrs. Anderson asked.

"I like our little plan," Mrs. Marshall replied with a smile. She pulled a sheet out of a manila folder that held a stack of papers and said, "In fact, I just learned something that will help it along! I think this just might work."

"Can't hurt!"

"We shall see."

Mrs. Anderson winked and went on her way while Mrs. Marshall placed the paper back in a folder labeled MATHCOUNTS and tucked it into her top desk drawer.

12

Alex was in her room working at her desk when her mother and sister returned home.

Mrs. Martinez stopped in to ask about her day. As she left she said, "Lights out in 30 minutes," and went to her room to change her clothes.

About 45 minutes later she returned to find Alex still up, reading in bed. "Sweetheart, it is time to go to bed. What is it you're reading?"

"Mom, have you ever heard of Grace Larrinua Lieblein? She's amazing, and she's Hispanic. Her father's family fled Cuba after Castro took over and they left with just what they were wearing. Can you believe that? It's almost like dad's family. But she still became really successful. It's a really good story, but the best part is that it's true!"

"This sounds like a good story, Alexandra."

"It says she became the first Hispanic female Global Vehicle Chief Engineer at GM."

"My, my, General Motors, that's very impressive. Why don't you close your book now and get to bed?"

"She said that sometimes she felt like she didn't fit in when she was away at school because she was a Hispanic woman, and there were mostly men studying to be engineers, and she got homesick and wondered if she could really make it. But she did."

"I'm glad there was a happy ending."

"Her father told her that everything can be taken away from you except for your education."

"Now this sounds just like what your father would say," Mrs. Martinez sat on the edge of the bed with her daughter.

"She says her mom raised her to believe that she could do anything."

"Oh sweetheart, so can you. There are no limits to what you can become. Listen to your heart, not to those who try to put boundaries on who you are and who you can be."

"Don't you expect me to be a cleaning lady, too?"

"Cleaning homes and offices is a fine job. But it's not what I expect to do for the rest of my life. I'm saving up money to one day follow through on your father's and my dream of owning a restaurant. And I don't expect you to be a cleaning lady. It's not what you are meant to be."

"Really?"

"Alexandra, you can be whatever you dream to be. It doesn't matter what everyone else thinks. Anything can happen in your world. But you must be ready to take advantage of the opportunity when it comes, and be ready to work hard. You have to make up your mind, and then go after it with all your heart."

Alex laughed out loud.

"What makes you laugh?"

"I think I heard those words before, Mom. I think I said them today. I just didn't realize I was talking about myself."

"They are true words, and you have more support than you know, from your sister, from me and from your teachers."

Alex looked down and said, "Mrs. Anderson gave me the information about Mrs. Lieblein today. I think maybe she knew I'd like the story."

"I think you'd be surprised about how much your teachers know. Now how about lights out and you can dream about this story tonight?"

"Okay, I will. I love you, Mom."

"I love you, too, sweetheart."

13

The next morning, Alex ran down the steps, greeted her mother who was putting dishes away, poured herself a bowl of cereal and ate while she wrote in her notebook.

Danielle came in, prepared a bowl of cereal and sliced a banana, arranging sections on top.

"Good morning!" Alex said cheerily.

Danielle stopped what she was doing and looked at Alex. "Good morning," she said slowly, almost suspiciously.

Alex finished her cereal, washed her dishes and started to leave the kitchen when she turned and examined Danielle's outfit.

"What?" Danielle felt her sister's gaze.

"Nothing." Alex turned to go, hesitated and asked, "Does this top look okay?"

"No," her sister replied flatly.

"So what, I like it."

Alex dashed upstairs, came back down a minute later, grabbed her backpack and kissed her mom goodbye.

"You changed your shirt," Danielle pointed out.

"Yep."

Danielle looked at her mother with a quizzical expression and asked, "Where is my sister and who is this girl?"

"See ya!" Alex waved a hand and was off.

~ ~ ~

The school day flew by, and for the first time, Alex looked forward to English class. After the students got seated, Mrs. Anderson asked, "Who would like to read his or her Women of Achievement report first?"

The room became quiet and students tried not to make eye contact for fear of being selected.

"Anyone?"

Alex raised her hand. "I will," she said with confidence.

There were snickers as some thought this was a practical joke, but Mrs. Anderson replied without hesitation, "Thank you, Alex."

Alex stood up, feeling the gaze of her classmates, and began. "I wrote about Grace Larrinua Lieblein. She's Hispanic." Alex glanced at Mrs. Anderson, then added, "Just like me." Mrs. Anderson smiled with a nod of encouragement. Alex read her report out loud, telling about Mrs. Lieblein's background, courage, perseverance and success. After a few minutes, she concluded, "What I learned is that a good education is important to become successful. People can try to knock you down, but that's one thing they can never take away from you."

The class applauded politely as Alex took her seat. She looked down to hide her wide grin.

~ ~ ~

Alex took her time walking home from school that afternoon. She had gotten used to being at detention and watching the silly math team worry over their problems, but she had served her "time" and no longer had to stay after school. It would be a little strange not being in Mrs. Marshall's class in the afternoons.

Mr. Fillion was nowhere in sight, so she stopped by the pet store and knelt at the window. Her heart sank when she saw only two of the kittens left. They had grown quite a bit over the last month into what she considered "junior cats."

"So your brothers and sisters all found homes," Alex talked softly through the window. "Don't worry, there will be a nice family who wants to take you home. I'd love to take you but my Mom says it wouldn't be fair to you since no one is home all day. I would take you, Miss Kitty…and if no one took your brother, I'd take…"

"They're cute!" Alex spun around to see who was speaking and was surprised to see Matt looking down at her.

"What are you doing here?" she questioned.

"Hi to you, too."

"Sorry, it's just…well, you don't live anywhere near here."

"I know, I saw you walking this way after school, and I wanted to tell you something."

"Okay, so tell me."

"I got cleared to play baseball at my physical yesterday."

"That's great news!"

"I know," Matt said with hesitation. "It's like you said, anything can happen."

"What's the matter? You don't sound so sure."

"I won't be able to be on the math team *and* the baseball team."

"Yeah, that's tough. What are you going to do?"

"I really don't want to let the math team down, and competition starts soon."

"And so…," Alex encouraged him to continue.

"So I thought about what you said, and you were right. This is that opportunity. I really want to play baseball. That's my dream. I'm going to do it."

"I think you're making a good choice, Matt."

"Thanks, that's what I thought you would say."

"It doesn't really matter what I think…it's

just important that you made the best choice for you."

"Well...," Matt smiled, "it kinda does matter what you think."

"Why?"

"See, if I leave the team, that leaves a spot open."

"So?"

"So, the rules say the person who has the next highest score from the School Competition can take my place."

"That sounds fair. So just go talk to him."

"I am."

"You are what?"

"Talking to him...well, her."

"What do you mean?"

"It's you."

"Me?"

"Yes, you."

"Oh." Alex paused and looked at Matt with a quizzical expression. "How can that be?"

"Mrs. Marshall scored your competition paper after all. In fact, if she had scored yours sooner, you probably would have been on the team, but you said you didn't want to be."

"She scored my paper?"

"Yeah, she scored your paper."

"So I did okay?"

"You did better than okay."

"So why'd she score my paper?"

"I think Mrs. Anderson had something to do with it."

"Mrs. Anderson?" Alex repeated.

"You should take my place." Matt ignored her question and tried to make his point.

"Are you kidding? Me, on the math team? I can't."

"Why not?"

"I just can't."

"Well, at least think about it. Mrs. Marshall says to stop in to see her before the team meets on Thursday if you are interested."

"Why are *you* telling me?"

"'Cause I asked Mrs. Marshall if I could."

Alex turned away and looked at the kittens in silence.

"At least think about it, okay?" Matt coaxed Alex.

"Okay."

"Okay," Matt confirmed.

Matt turned and started to walk toward the school. A few seconds later, Alex turned and called out after him, "Good luck playing baseball!"

Without turning around, he gave her a "thumbs up" and yelled, "Good luck on the math team!"

I wonder why she scored my competition paper?

Alex thought to herself. She pictured herself on the team: sharpened pencil, a blue blazer with a school emblem, coming home with a trophy. She smiled and gazed into the window of the pet store and caught a glimpse of her reflection. Her face fell. *What was I thinking?* She held her hand up to the window and Miss Kitty stretched up her front legs to meet it. "Goodnight, Miss Kitty."

14

Emily came into homeroom the next morning like a tornado, dropped her books on her desk and exclaimed for anyone to hear, "Oh my gosh, did you hear that Matt quit the team?"

"I can't believe it, no one has ever quit before," Sarah agreed.

"He's just nuts." Emily proclaimed.

"Just nuts!" Sarah nodded.

"He's a good ball player. It's his dream," Alex piped in.

"Oh, well that's good that he follows his dream," Sarah agreed.

Emily spun around to see who was disagreeing, darted Alex a disapproving glare and shot Sarah the same.

"But overall, just nuts." Sarah corrected.

"How do they fill the spot?" Earl asked. Like Sarah, Earl attended the practices, but was not selected for the competition team.

The three looked at each other, each thinking the other might have the answer.

Sarah shrugged her shoulders. Emily searched for her rule book in her backpack while Earl fiddled with his pen.

"The person whose score is the next highest from the School Competition is offered the spot," Alex offered.

Emily let out an exaggerated groan and continued looking through her rule book, ignoring Alex's input.

"Here it is!" Emily announced, keeping her gaze on the book. "The person who scores next highest on the School Competition is offered the position."

"Isn't that what Alex said?" Sarah questioned meekly.

"Well, it was similar, but not exactly as the rule book stated," Emily corrected.

Sarah and Earl exchanged glances. Sarah shrugged her shoulders again.

"Wow, this is exciting," Earl said. "I wonder who it will be. I would love to be on the team, wouldn't you, Alex?"

For a second she felt a flash of excitement well up inside as she saw Earl's and Sarah's enthusiastic faces. Then she caught a glimpse of Emily staring at her in mock disbelief. She composed herself and said indifferently, "Uh, I don't think so," emphasizing each word with distinction. Earl's face fell.

Emily just had to keep this going. "Even if Alex finished the test, which I doubt she did, what would the point be?"

"What's that supposed to mean?" Alex felt her temper rising.

"Well, it's simple," Emily explained. "What's someone like you need to care about math, or for that matter, school? Her mom is a cleaning lady, her sister is a cleaning lady. Three guesses what Alex is going to be."

Sarah gasped. Earl watched blankly and made a calculation, "A cleaning lady?"

"Bingo!" Emily concluded.

Alex felt her throat tighten and her eyes smart with the threat of tears. She remained motionless for what seemed like an eternity. The shrill sound of the homeroom bell broke the horrible spell.

~ ~ ~

Later that day, Alex entered the cafeteria and made her way to her usual table. Kit arrived seconds later, glanced around the table and asked, "Where's Matt?"

"He came to his senses and quit the math team and is back on the baseball team," Brian said. "He's over there," he continued as he pointed toward the "jock" table where Matt was the center of attention.

Funny how they all want to be his friend again, Alex thought. She finished her lunch quietly, gathered her things and made her way out of the cafeteria. As she passed Matt's table, he looked at her and paused as if about to say something, but he was interrupted by one of his teammates who slapped him on the back and said, "Welcome back to the team, buddy!"

Alex wandered out into the hall toward her locker. She passed Mrs. Marshall's room, then turned back and knocked on the open door. "Excuse me, Mrs. Marshall," she said. "May I talk to you for a minute?"

15

The following afternoon, when Emily walked into Mrs. Marshall's room for math team practice, Alex avoided making eye contact.

"Detention again?" Emily said cheerily with an annoying flip of her hair.

Her taunting was short-lived as Mrs. Marshall announced that it was time to issue team shirts. Emily quickly took her seat.

"David." As Mrs. Marshall called out their names, each competition team member walked up to her desk to be awarded an official team shirt. The remaining team members clapped for David, Janella and Emily.

"As you all may now know," Mrs. Marshall explained, "Matt was presented with the opportunity to play ball again this spring and has decided to pursue that. We wish him the best of luck. Please welcome our newest MATHCOUNTS member, Alex Martinez." A blanket of silence fell over the room. Alex approached her teacher feeling the gaze of every eye in the room on her.

"Please welcome Alex," Mrs. Marshall repeated. The students started to clap.

"I object!" a voice rang out.

"Emily, did you say something?" The room quieted.

"I object," Emily stated with confidence.

"Pardon me, Emily, but to what, may I ask, do you object?" Mrs. Marshall inquired.

"The rules say that the person who fills a missing slot has to have the next highest score, which means Alex would have had to have the fifth highest score on the competition."

"Ahh, you are correct, Emily, Alex did not have the fifth highest score on the competition."

Emily smiled contentedly as if saying *case closed*, as Alex flushed with embarrassment.

"She had the *highest* score," Mrs. Marshall announced with finality. "Congratulations, Alex, and welcome to the team."

A wave of relief rushed over Alex, and she retrieved her team shirt.

"Way to go, Alex," David said and shook her hand.

Alex stood silently, overwhelmed by the shower of attention from the other students who crowded around offering congratulations.

Emily sat stunned in disbelief.

~ ~ ~

Thoughts were racing through Alex's mind as she walked home after school. She stopped to visit

Miss Kitty, kneeling to watch her favorite cat trot up to the window to meet her.

"Guess what?" Alex asked out loud.

Miss Kitty meowed as if responding on cue.

"I'm on the math team at school," Alex explained to the cat. "Yep, silly ol' me. I have an official shirt and everything." She paused to see Miss Kitty's reaction. The little cat pranced over to her food dish, nibbled a few morsels, then curled up in a ball in the corner.

"I see you are excited about my news. To tell you the truth, I think I'm a little over my head." Alex had been staring blankly through the glass when she got the feeling someone was watching her. She noticed Mr. Fillion standing in the door of the shop and gasped.

"Hello, young lady," he said.

"Oh!" Alex jumped to her feet as her heartbeat quickened. She stared at him in confused surprise and finally blurted out, "Hi." She quickly turned to leave, tripped over a crack in the sidewalk and hastily headed home.

Mr. Fillion chuckled, put the *Closed* sign on the door and turned out the lights in the shop.

~ ~ ~

Mrs. Martinez and Danielle returned home that evening with a bag of doughnuts, and the three enjoyed a snack before bed.

"How was your day, Alexandra?" Mrs. Martinez inquired.

"Fine."

"Anything new?"

Alex hesitated as she considered the day's events. "No."

"That's it?" Danielle prodded. "Nothing happened all day?"

Alex considered telling them about the team but was afraid. Danielle would probably give her grief, and what if she couldn't keep up with the rest of the team? Instead she said, "Mr. Fillion talked to me."

"Mr. Fillion, the old pet guy?" Danielle asked in disbelief.

"Yeah."

"He's nuts."

"Danielle!" Mrs. Martinez scolded. "Mr. Fillion has been in the neighborhood for years. He's a good businessman."

"He scares me," Danielle insisted.

"Me, too," Alex agreed.

"So, no more detention Alexandra?"

"No, Mom, no more."

"I expect you to come straight home from school every day and do your homework."

"Of course," she lied.

"That's my good girl."

Danielle got up from the table and announced, "I'm headed up to do my homework." As she passed her sister, she stopped, squeezed Alex's cheeks between her fingers, and mimicking her mother, said, "That's my good girl." She tousled Alex's hair and ran.

Alex jumped out of her seat, nearly knocking it over, and chased her up the stairs as both girls giggled all the way to their room. Mrs. Martinez called to them to be careful, but neither heard her.

Once in their room, Danielle pulled a book from her backpack and sat on her bed to read. Alex put her backpack on her bed and unzipped it to get her homework folder. Folded neatly on top was her MATHCOUNTS team shirt. She ran her fingers over the top of it and thought about the moment she received it.

"Whatcha got there?" Danielle asked, trying to see what Alex had in her hands. Alex quickly bunched the shirt into a ball and stuffed it under her pillow.

"Nothing," she replied. "Mind your own business."

"Excuse me, Miss Touchy."

Alex grabbed her folder, sat down at her desk, picked up her pencil, glanced at her pillow and smiled to herself.

16

Tuesday afternoon was Alex's first official MATHCOUNTS practice. The competition team members were seated together at the front of the room while the rest of the students were scattered in the seats behind them.

"Our preliminary competition is in only one week," Mrs. Marshall explained. "So we are going to do a number of drills to help sharpen your skills. The idea is to work together as a team and submit an answer you all agree on. I'll present a problem and start the timer. You may use paper, pencil and a calculator if necessary." She opened her drawer, took out a chrome bell and placed it toward the edge of her desk. "Determine the answer, then any team member may ring the bell to announce it."

Question 1: A stock's price starts at $10 on January 1, 2004. Each January 1 its price is exactly 10% more than it was the previous January 1. What is its price on January 1, 2007?

The room fell silent. Emily immediately began writing a list of numbers. David and Janella picked up their calculators. The other team members worked diligently at their desks. The shrill ring of the bell caused all work to come to a screeching halt. All eyes turned toward their teacher, then searched to see who had rung the bell.

"Alex," Mrs. Marshall politely corrected, "you are only to ring the bell once your team has the answer."

"I told you it was a mistake letting her on the team," Emily whispered to Janella just loud enough to be overheard. Janella nodded in agreement.

"The answer is $13.31," Alex said flatly.

"That is correct, Alex. Well done." A wave of whispers spread across the room. "Next problem."

Question 2: Veronica ate a total of 100 jellybeans in five days. Each day after the first day she ate six more than she had eaten on the previous day. How many jellybeans did she eat on the third day?

The students attacked the problem with enthusiasm. Within seconds, the bell rang out.

"Alex?" Mrs. Marshall called on her.

"Twenty," she replied.

"Wow! That's just amazing," Sarah called out.

"That is correct," Mrs. Marshall confirmed. "Let's remember to work as a team," she firmly said, looking at Alex. Emily raised her hand, then started waving it to catch Mrs. Marshall's attention.

"Yes, Emily?" Mrs. Marshall called on her.

"Jellybeans."

"I beg your pardon?" Mrs. Marshall questioned.

"It's twenty *jellybeans*," she explained. "Alex forgot to say jellybeans."

The teacher looked at her blankly for a moment, then continued, "Jellybeans. Thank you, Emily. Shall we move on to the next question?"

Emily smiled and poised her pencil for the next problem.

As Alex proceeded to answer each question correctly, her confidence grew. No sooner did Mrs. Marshall ask the question, than Alex rang the bell and delivered the right answer. After practice, the team members crowded around, congratulating her on her ability. Emily stood to the side, not used to the lack of attention.

"Can you believe Alex got every question right?" Sarah asked no one in particular.

"It's not really such a big deal," Emily corrected. "It's just beginner's luck. Besides, she doesn't know how to be a team player. She's supposed to check the answer with us first."

"Who cares? She's so fast, it's amazing," Sarah continued with admiration and left to congratulate the new star.

"She's going to ruin the team," Emily called after her, but Sarah had already caught up with the crowd around Alex.

~ ~ ~

At Thursday's practice, Alex continued to dominate, swiftly answering each problem correctly and gaining admiration from her teammates...most of her teammates.

"You're supposed to check your answer with us first," Emily reprimanded.

Alex responded with a look that said, *big deal.*

"It really doesn't matter, Emily," David said. "Who cares as long as she gets it right for us? We're going to win."

"It does matter," Emily complained. "We're supposed to be working as a team."

"I think you are all ready for our first practice competition next Tuesday against East Middle School," Mrs. Marshall announced. "Keep practicing and remember to wear your shirts. We will meet in the cafeteria at 4pm." The students packed up their belongings and filed out of the classroom.

17

On Tuesday morning, Alex stopped by her locker to drop off her books.

"Alex," Janella called out as she approached her. Janella proudly wore her blue and gold MATHCOUNTS t-shirt and a pair of khaki pants. "Where is your t-shirt? Did you forget?"

"I didn't forget."

"Then why aren't you wearing it?"

"It's bad enough that I'm on the team, but I'm not going to take grief all day by broadcasting it."

"Oh," Janella's face fell. "See you at the competition," she said as she turned to head off to class.

"Yeah, see ya." Alex shut her locker and went to class.

~ ~ ~

At lunch, Alex was surprised to have Matt take the empty seat next to her.

"I thought you moved up in the world and didn't sit at this table any more," Alex said without looking at him.

"That's right, I don't," he agreed. "I thought I'd brighten everyone's day."

"Funny."

"Isn't your first round of competition today?" he asked.

"It's just a practice competition against East."

"East? Didn't they beat us out of going to the State Competition last year?"

"So?"

"So, good luck."

"No luck necessary. This will be a cinch."

Matt raised his eyebrows at her response. "Anyway, have fun."

"Right," she replied sarcastically. She pulled a peanut butter and jelly sandwich out of her bag and started eating.

"Uh, I gotta go," Matt said abruptly.

Alex watched with surprise as he packed up his lunch and moved to another table.

So what? Alex thought, and finished her sandwich in silence.

～ ～ ～

As soon as the last bell rang, Alex made her way to the cafeteria for the practice competition. Two tables were set about 20 feet apart with four folding chairs placed behind each. About two dozen additional chairs were set up for a small audience. Someone had written the school names in neat block letters on poster board and attached one to the front of each table. Her teammates were already there working on practice problems.

"You're late," Emily said flatly.

"I'm here, aren't I?" Alex replied.

"Did you forget your shirt?"

Alex unzipped her sweatshirt to reveal a wrinkled team shirt, posed for Emily, then zipped it back up.

Mrs. Marshall entered the room smiling and greeted the visiting team, encouraging her students to do the same. Alex took a seat and watched while the students mingled and helped themselves to small cups of apple juice and pretzels.

A teacher from East with salt and pepper hair and a mustache to match stood up and explained the competition rules. "Good luck," he said, and the contest began. The students worked on individual problems in the first rounds, and the score was tied when it came time for the Team Countdown Round where each side worked simultaneously to arrive at an answer. The first question was announced:

Two 12-hour clocks each start at exactly 6 o'clock. One clock loses one minute every hour, and the other clock gains one minute every hour. In how many days will the clocks first show the same time as each other again?

"We should use calculators," Emily directed.

Tension mounted as the minutes passed. The students from both schools were scrambling to arrive at the answer when Alex's hand came down on the bell.

"West?" The moderator called out. "Your answer, please?"

"Fifteen," Alex said.

Emily looked up in disbelief.

Alex looked Emily right in the eye and added the word "days."

"That is correct."

The team members and those in the audience clapped with approval.

"Check with us first, Alex," Emily scolded.

"Question two," announced the moderator while the students listened intently.

The opposing team's bell rang almost at the same time that Alex's hand hit the bell.

"East, may we have your answer please?"

"The answer is x equals 4," a member from the opposing team announced.

"Correct."

"Wait for the team to agree to an answer," Emily demanded so everyone could hear.

"The next correct answer will determine the match," the moderator announced and delivered the final question. The air was heavy with tension as the students scribbled on their scratch pads.

Alex's hand slammed down on the bell, breaking the silence.

"West, your answer please."

All eyes were on Alex as she said, "The answer is 18 dollars per day."

"That is incorrect." A wave of whispers rolled over the room.

"East, do you have the answer?" the moderator inquired.

The students from East bowed their heads close together and a member responded, "The answer is 20 dollars per day."

"That is correct. East Middle School is the winner of our first practice competition. Congratulations, and we look forward to meeting again at the Chapter Competition." A round of polite applause rang out and the team members exchanged handshakes, except for Alex who grabbed her sweatshirt and headed for her locker. Emily saw her leaving and ran after her.

"Alex!" Emily called after her. "Thanks for nothing!" Alex continued walking, ignoring the comment.

"You're ruining the team," Emily continued.

Swinging around abruptly, Alex turned to confront Emily. "If I didn't answer, we wouldn't have even scored a point."

Mrs. Marshall came into the hallway and

caught up to the girls. "Excuse me, Alex, may I speak with you for a moment?"

"Thank you, Mrs. Marshall," Emily said smugly. "She's just not a team player. I don't mean to say anything, but I said this was going to happen."

"Thank you, Emily. Would you kindly excuse us?"

"Oh," Emily said in surprise. She looked at Alex with a knowing look and went to her locker. Alex cringed, expecting the worst.

"So, how is it going, Alex?" Mrs. Marshall asked.

"Fine." They walked together in silence.

"I was wondering if you could stay after school for the next few days."

"Mrs. Marshall, I don't understand. It wasn't my fault that we lost," Alex defended herself. "This is unfair. I shouldn't have to stay after school."

"While your behavior might not have been the best for our team, that's not why I stopped you," Mrs. Marshall explained. "I just thought that since you've been working harder this semester, I can give you some extra credit to pull up your math grade to where it should be. And I could use your help with something if you can stop by my classroom after school for the next few days."

Alex thought about the offer. With a little extra credit, she could probably bring her grade up to an A. "Sure," she said casually. "What is it you want me to do?"

"Why don't I just explain it tomorrow afternoon?"

18

The next day after school, Alex stopped in to see Mrs. Marshall. She was sitting on a small chair that was pulled up next to one of the desks. A slender little girl was sitting at the desk. She wore a sweatshirt that had the Chicago Cubs baseball team logo across the front and a pair of worn jeans. Her light brown hair was pulled back into a braid that had become loose during the day. Freckles dotted her nose and cheeks, and she furrowed her brow as she studied the paper in front of her. Alex guessed that she was about eight years old.

"Alex!" Mrs. Marshall greeted her. "I'm glad you made it. I want to introduce you to Ronna."

"Hey," Alex casually nodded to the little girl.

Ronna continued to study the piece of paper and without looking up said, "Hey," almost copying Alex's tone.

"Ronna is in third grade at Aurora Elementary. Her mother signed her up for our after-school math tutoring program with Mrs. Button, the 8th grade math teacher, but she just went out on maternity leave. I suggested we could have a student help out till the end of the month when Mrs. Button's replacement can take over. I just knew you would be interested."

Alex looked blankly at Mrs. Marshall as she tried to absorb what she just heard. She looked at the little girl and then back at Mrs. Marshall.

"Great!" Mrs. Marshall said as if sealing the deal. "Let's get started. Ronna does very well on state testing, but for some reason has fallen behind in math class. She has gotten Ds on her last two tests, and her mother asked for some help. Her next test is in just eight days, so we thought with a little extra work, she might be able to do better. I hoped that you could meet with her after school till then and help her with her multiplication and percentages."

"Well, um, I don't know anything about teaching math."

"Oh, I'm sure you will do a great job. Okay, you two, have fun! I'll be back in 30 minutes."

Alex watched Mrs. Marshall leave the room, not entirely believing what just happened. She looked down at Ronna and wondered what to do next. Ronna was scribbling something on the desk.

"Hey!" Alex snapped.

"Hey yourself."

"Stop that," Alex demanded.

"Stop that," Ronna mimicked.

"Come on, stop writing on the desk."

"And do what?"

Alex looked around the room as if in search of an answer. "Um, I don't know. I guess you have to work on your multiplication tables and percentages."

"Are you going to teach them to me?"

"It looks that way."

"So teach me."

"Well, okay. Um. What do you know?"

"I know I'm bored. I know you're a bad teacher. I know I'd rather be home playing video games."

Alex's face flushed and her temper started to rise.

"Okay, let's start with the two tables. What's two times two?"

"22."

"Are you kidding?"

"What do you think?"

Alex stiffened and let out a loud, long breath.

"Okay, how about we try again?"

"Why should *we* try, don't you already know how to multiply?"

"Okay, you try."

For the next 15 minutes, Alex felt like she was going in circles trying to get Ronna to pay attention. Finally Mrs. Marshall returned to the room. Alex was never so happy to see her teacher.

"How is it going, girls?" Mrs. Marshall inquired.

"Very well, Mrs. Marshall," Ronna replied sweetly.

"Good, same time tomorrow, then?"

"Okay, bye." Ronna said as she went out to meet her mother who was waiting in the hallway.

"How did it go?" Mrs. Marshall asked.

"Not too well. I don't think I taught her a thing. She doesn't pay attention, she doesn't even try."

"I'm sure you will think of something, Alex. Remember we have a MATHCOUNTS practice after school tomorrow. Why don't you meet with Ronna, then come right over to practice? We will be in the cafeteria."

Perfect, Alex thought as she gathered her things. *I'm supposed to think of something.* She couldn't get out the door fast enough.

19

Thursday afternoon's session seemed like a carbon copy of the first day. Ronna doodled on her notebook and tuned Alex out for the majority of the 30 minutes. After Ronna left to meet her mother, Alex approached Mrs. Marshall.

"Mrs. Marhsall, I think this is just a waste of time. Ronna doesn't listen to me, and I can't teach her a thing. I feel horrible."

"Well, that could be a problem with her test just seven days from now."

"She just doesn't like math."

"Good point, Alex. It makes you wonder what she *does* like, doesn't it? I'll see you tomorrow."

How did I get myself into this? Alex wondered. *And who cares what she likes?*

~ ~ ~

Friday afternoon went no better, and by Monday, Alex dreaded meeting with Ronna. *What was with that little girl? Didn't she care about her grades or what anyone thought?* Alex felt unappreciated. She walked in just as Mrs. Marshall was walking out. "Good afternoon, Alex," Mrs. Marshall said cheerily as she passed.

Alex set her face sternly as she approached

Ronna, who was doodling on her hand in pen. She wore faded jeans, a sweatshirt and a Cubs baseball cap.

"Knock it off."

Ronna put her pen down and showed Alex her best bored expression.

"Okay, let's see the paper for learning threes that I gave you Friday to work on."

"You mean this one?" Ronna asked as she pulled a crumpled sheet out of her backpack. Nothing was filled in.

"Yeah, that one. Is there a reason you left it blank?"

"Um, let me think." She paused and looked into the air, then back at Alex. "No."

"Is there anything you want to tell me?" Alex searched for an apology from the little girl.

Ronna sat quietly and thought. "Yeah, I guess so."

"What is it?"

"Your hair is a mess."

Alex tried not to lose her cool. "Would you take that baseball cap off? It's not polite to wear it inside."

Ronna pulled her cap off and tossed it next to her book bag that had the same Cubs logo.

"You a Cubs fan?"

"Duh."

"Yeah, guess so." Alex quickly tried to collect her thoughts. "Okay, then. Let's say you wanted to figure out a batting average, do you know how to do that?"

"Of course I do. You take how many times the player makes a hit out of how many times he's up at bat."

"What do you mean?" Alex encouraged. "Give me an example."

"It's like this. Let's say a player is up 60 times and he makes 30 hits. Then his average is .500. That would be unbelievably awesome."

"So that would be like 50%?"

"Exactly," Ronna confirmed.

"I think I get it. Can you give me another example?"

"Oh brother, you're thick. Okay…a guy is up 80 times at bat and he hits 20 times. Then he's got a .250 average. I'd trade him!" Ronna laughed and Alex smiled.

".250," Alex considered. "So would that be like saying he got a hit 25% of the time he was up at bat?"

"Duh, yeah."

"So," Alex added, "let's say that I had $80, and I spent $20, what percent of the total did I spend?"

"What?"

"Come on, what percent of the total did I spend?"

"I dunno."

"Figure it out like a batting average," Alex encouraged.

Ronna looked at her as if she was clueless, then a smile crossed her face, and she said, ".250 or 25%!"

"That's right," Alex praised her, "Let's try another one."

The two worked on problems for the next ten minutes and were working intently when Mrs. Marshall came in.

"Excuse me for interrupting, but Ronna's mother is here."

"Wait! I've got one more," Ronna commanded eagerly. "60%!" she announced.

"That's right," Alex said.

Ronna and Alex slapped their hands together in a high-five.

"See ya tomorrow," Ronna said as she gathered up her belongings.

"See ya," Alex replied.

"Girls, we have our second MATHCOUNTS practice competition tomorrow against Moon Middle School, so I'm afraid we will have to skip a day of tutoring," Mrs. Marshall explained.

"No big deal," Ronna said.

Mrs. Marshall detected her disappointment, even though she acted like it didn't matter. "Ronna, if your mom would like to bring you over, you may watch the competition."

"Okay, maybe," Ronna replied without committing.

~ ~ ~

Alex felt as if she had really gotten through to Ronna and her head was filled with ideas about how to keep her interested and excited about math. She was feeling good about herself and looked forward to sharing her news with Miss Kitty. But when she came upon the plate glass window at the pet shop, she could not find her furry friend.

"Miss Kitty," she called out softly as she tapped on the glass. "Where are you? Are you hiding?" She started to worry that Miss Kitty wasn't there.

Suddenly she noticed Mr. Fillion standing at the door.

"She's no longer for sale, miss."

Alex's heart sank. Miss Kitty was gone. She would never be her cat.

"I'm sorry, miss."

"That's okay." Alex stared blankly into the empty window.

"You really like animals, don't you?"

"I do, especially cats."

"You are Mr. Martinez's daughter, aren't you?"

"Yes, did you know my dad?"

"Yes, I knew him well. He was a good man."

Feeling uncomfortable, Alex looked down at her feet and wanted to go.

"We are looking for help on a few afternoons after school," Mr. Fillion added. "Would you be interested in some part-time work?"

"What would I do?"

"You would help stock products on the shelves, make sure the animals have fresh water, and eventually, I could teach you to run the register."

Wow, a real job, Alex thought. "I'll ask my mom."

"How are your grades?"

Alex cringed, knowing that her grades could be better. She suddenly wished she had worked harder at school. "Um, they're pretty good," she replied.

"I'll get you an application. If you decide you want to work, fill it out and drop it off tomorrow."

"If it's okay with you, can I wait till the middle of next week to start? I kinda have something to do after school for a week or so."

"That's fine." He handed her an application.

Alex thanked Mr. Fillion and turned to leave. She skipped home, brimming with enthusiasm.

That evening, Alex mentioned the job offer, which pleased her mother.

"This is a very good thing, Alexandra." They decided that she could work two days a week after school. Mrs. Martinez helped her fill out the application. "When does he want you to start?" she inquired.

"Uh, tomorrow, he has some really important stuff he needs help with as soon as possible," Alex replied, crossing her fingers behind her back.

"So soon?" her mother considered it. "Yes, I think this will work as long as you keep up with your homework."

This made everything perfect. Now she didn't have to tell her mom about staying after school or about the competition. She decided she really wasn't lying.

"Tomorrow?" Danielle questioned. "That's awfully fast. Don't you have to have an interview or something first?"

"Well, I had to fill out the application."

"And you start tomorrow?"

"Yes," Alex lied.

"It's wonderful, and I'm proud of you," her mother said and stroked the top of her head.

"Boy am I tired," Alex announced. "I think I'll go up to bed." She kissed her mother goodnight, and slipped out of the room as quickly as possible.

Once she was safely in her room, she looked into her mirror and thought, *What have I gotten myself into now?*

20

The next morning, Alex slipped into her MATHCOUNTS t-shirt and pulled her hoodie over it to hide it. She grabbed a quick breakfast and headed to school. When she arrived at homeroom, she was greeted by Emily and a few of the team members.

"The team has asked me to say a few words to you," Emily announced.

"So say them."

"Alex, a big part of MATHCOUNTS is working as a team. You can't just keep shouting out answers. The goal of our team is to win, and we all help each other. You aren't acting like part of the team. So maybe it would be best if you just aren't part of the team, get it?"

"Yeah, I get it."

Mrs. Anderson walked in and the kids scattered to their seats.

~ ~ ~

That afternoon, Alex was surprised to see a few more people in the audience for the competition. Sarah's mother was sitting there. She spotted Mr. and Mrs. Liu, and then she saw Matt.

"What are you doing here?" Alex asked.

"Glad to see you, too," Matt smiled in response. "I just thought I'd come out to see what I'm missing."

"Not a whole lot, trust me."

"I'll be the judge of that."

"Prepare to be dazzled."

"I'd better be."

"Well, to tell you the truth…"

Alex was cut short by the sugary voice of Emily, "Why hello, Matt. I'm glad you came."

Matt turned his attention away from Alex and smiled at Emily. Her hair was shiny and curled and neatly tucked back in a pretty headband. Her t-shirt was pressed and tucked into khaki pants with a matching cloth belt. Alex stepped away and unzipped her hoodie. Her t-shirt still was wrinkled from being stashed under her pillow, and she wore it loosely over her faded jeans. She pulled some strands of hair and tried to anchor them behind her ears without success and sauntered to her seat.

After Mrs. Marshall welcomed Moon Middle School and one of the officials reviewed the rules, the second practice competition was under way. The students sat at attention with their pencils poised, ready for the first round of questions. As they moved into the Team Countdown Round, the official reminded them how the round would work and finished by saying, "And remember you may work together. Any team member may ring the bell to announce the answer. Good luck! Here is your first team problem."

What is the sum of the total values of every possible combination of three coins using only pennies, nickels, dimes and quarters?

After the team worked on the problem for a few minutes, Emily took command, "Okay, I think..."

DING!

"West? Do you have an answer?" the official asked.

"The answer is $6.15," Alex announced.

"That is correct."

Alex flashed a fake smile at Emily and glanced at Matt. He gave her a "thumbs-up." She felt her confidence swell.

"Next question," the official announced.

Once again, Alex jumped to ring the bell.

"West?" the announcer called out.

"The answer is 18," Alex called out as she winked at Emily.

"That is incorrect. Moon, do you have an answer?"

"The answer is 9," replied a girl wearing a headband that matched her uniform.

"That is correct."

Alex tapped her foot nervously. Emily shot her a stern look. The official announced the next question and Alex's hand shot to the bell. She looked directly at Emily as she blurted out the answer.

"Incorrect," responded the official. Alex felt her face flush.

After a brief break to calculate the score, the announcer named Moon the winner. "Congratulations, Moon Middle School. This concludes the rounds of this practice competition. We look forward to seeing your teams join four others from the area at the Chapter Competition in February. The winning team will advance to the State Competition in March."

The West students shook hands with their opponents and filed out quickly. No one made eye contact with Alex, and that's exactly what she wanted. She decided to cheer herself by talking to Matt, but he was already walking out of the cafeteria with Emily. Ronna and her mother came up to her.

"Oh, you came," Alex said with surprise.

"That was a very interesting competition, Alex," Ronna's mom said politely, then went off to get some cookies that were arranged on one of the tables. Ronna and Alex stood next to each other in silence.

"Bummer, huh?" Ronna finally said.

"Yeah, bummer."

"Maybe you shouldn't try to do everything yourself."

"Yeah, maybe."

"See you tomorrow."

"Okay."

Alex wandered home. She was happy to be there. The familiar smell of tomato sauce filled the house and she felt safe and warm.

"Alexandra, I'm in the kitchen," her mom called to her.

What is Mom doing home so early? she wondered and quickly zipped up her hoodie to hide her t-shirt.

Alex found her mom making meatballs at the counter.

"How was school today?"

"Fine," Alex replied. "Why are you home early?"

"The delicatessen I clean is closing, so I finished up early today. And how was your first day on the job?"

"The what?" Alex hesitated, then recoverd. "It was good." A wave of relief washed over her as she realized her mother thought she had been at Mr. Fillion's pet store.

"What did you do?"

"Oh, you know, counted boxes of cat food and filled water dishes. It was easy," she lied.

"Do you like it?"

"Sure," she replied. "The sauce smells great, Mom. I'm going to go start my homework."

"Okay, dinner will be ready in twenty minutes!"

21

When Ronna entered Mrs. Marshall's room the next afternoon she saw a big diamond drawn on the chalkboard.

"What's up?" Ronna asked Alex.

"Ready to practice some multiplication?"

"No."

"Okay, let's get started. Let's start with 8s."

"Ick."

"What's eight times eight?"

"66."

"Ooh, too bad, it's 64. Strike one," Alex said and put a hash mark on the board next to the diamond.

"What's that supposed to mean?"

"Isn't that how it works in baseball? You only have two strikes left, then I'm up at bat."

Ronna took another look at the diamond on the board and realized that they were playing baseball with multiplication.

"Ha! Lay one on me, and make it a fastball."

"Okay, eight times nine?"

Ronna furrowed her brow. "72!" she yelled out.

"That's not just a base hit, that's a double!" Alex

said and made an "x" at the top of the diamond indicating she was on second base.

Ronna smiled with delight as Alex called out, "Batter up!"

Mrs. Marshall smiled as she sat at her desk watching the girls. When it was time for Ronna's mother to pick her up, she reminded the girls that this was the last tutoring session. Tomorrow was Ronna's math exam, and Alex and Mrs. Marshall wished her luck. The little girl left, and they were alone in the classroom.

"Very nice job, Alex," Mrs. Marshall complimented her.

"Thank you, it was fun."

"You're a good teacher."

"I'm not a teacher."

"But you are. You showed Ronna how to discover capabilities she had all along."

"It's hard work, isn't it?"

"Yes it is. But it's rewarding, don't you think?"

"Yeah, I guess it is." Alex smiled.

"Alex, there's an old saying: 'Give a man a fish and he will eat for a day, teach a man to fish and he will eat for a lifetime.'"

"I'm sorry, I don't get it."

"Oh, but you will. I'll see you tomorrow at practice."

22

Alex arrived at MATHCOUNTS practice on Thursday after school just as Mrs. Marshall was closing the door to the classroom. Emily jumped to her feet when she entered the room and announced, "Mrs. Marshall, the team and I are asking to have Alex removed. She is ruining our chances to win."

"I see," Mrs. Marshall replied. Alex stood still, looking at the faces of the team members and feeling as if she could no longer breathe. "Since the competition is next week, we will keep the team exactly as it is."

"But if we don't win next week, we'll have to wait till next year to compete again," Emily pleaded.

"And I couldn't stand having East beat us two years in a row," David chimed in.

"I understand your concerns. And I understand that winning is important. That's why we've been practicing so hard. But there are also other important things that we are doing here. Learning to work together as a team is certainly one of them. Learning about leadership, how to help one another and how to respect each other are things

104

we can all stand to improve. Alex will remain on the team."

"That's okay, Mrs. Marshall, I'm quitting." Alex concluded. She grabbed her things and left abruptly.

Emily smiled with satisfaction. David looked at his feet sheepishly. Mrs. Marshall took a deep breath and exhaled slowly, picked up a stack of papers and handed out practice problems. The team members worked quietly until it was time to go home.

"Remember, we will have practice Monday afternoon before Tuesday's competition," Mrs. Marshall reminded the class. "Everyone rest up over the weekend."

23

In a sour mood and feeling like an outcast Monday morning, Alex was surprised when Mrs. Anderson delivered a note from Mrs. Marshall requesting her to stop by her room after school. She didn't want to see the team members, so she did her homework in the library, then waited outside the classroom until practice was over. Mrs. Marshall's voice was muffled behind the door, but she could hear her giving final instructions for the following day's competition as she dismissed the students.

The sound of footsteps in the hall diverted her attention away from the classroom and she saw Matt and two of his friends coming out of the gym walking her way. She quickly ducked into the girls' room doorway. Mrs. Marshall's door swung open, just in time for Emily to greet Matt. She flashed her best smile and called out his name with her sugary sweetness. Alex cringed.

"Hi there, Matt," she said.

Matt nodded, "Hey Emily. Good luck at the competition tomorrow."

"Will you be there?" Emily inquired, widening her grin.

"Sure."

"Do you think I can get a ride home with you today?"

"I'll ask my mom. It shouldn't be a problem."

Alex tried not to feel jealous, but she couldn't help it. She leaned against the cool wall until the halls became silent. When they were clear, she entered Mrs. Marshall's room.

"Hi, Mrs. Marshall, you asked to see me?" Alex inquired.

"Hello, Alex, I thought you might have forgotten to stop by this afternoon. We missed you at practice."

"Well, like I said, I quit the team."

"Yes, I know what you said. May I ask why?"

"It's obvious, isn't it? Everyone hates me. I don't know what I was thinking in the first place. I don't belong with the smart kids. They're all going to college. I don't think like them, I don't act like them and I sure don't belong with them."

"Alex, you are one of the smart kids, you just haven't recognized it yet," Mrs. Marshall observed. "You've come a long way in a short while. It would be a shame to quit now, but I'm not going to tell you what to do. You've got to do what is right for you. But this isn't the first time, and it certainly isn't the last time you are going to be up against a challenge. I know how you feel. I've faced a lot of uphill climbs over the years, especially as a teacher. There's a reason I became a teacher, and it all stems from some advice one of my teachers gave me when I was in a situation not so different from yours.

"You see, I was the first one in my family to go to college and I had a tough time working my way through school and keeping my grades up. Although I'd like to think we are beyond it, being a woman of color, I faced some issues of prejudice. Success didn't come easy to me. But something she told me stuck with me. She said, 'Knowledge is power, education is freedom.' Those are good words to live by. You are a smart girl. If you use your knowledge the right way, it will take you far."

"Thanks, Mrs. Marshall," Alex replied. "Is that what you wanted to tell me?"

Mrs. Marshall realized she hadn't gotten through to Alex. "No, I wanted to give this to you," she said as she handed her a large folded sheet of blue construction paper. "Ronna's mother dropped this off for you today."

Mrs. Marshall turned her attention back to her paperwork as Alex unfolded the sheet to reveal a white piece of paper cut like a diamond pasted on the blue construction paper. A Chicago Cubs logo was drawn at the top. She read the hand-

written message that was carefully centered on the
diamond:

> *Alex,*
>
> *I scored a homerun on my math test.
> Thank you. I didn't think I needed help from
> anyone. I guess I did. You made math fun.*
>
> *Your friend,*
> *Ronna*
> *P.S. Go Cubs!*

Alex stared at the words and repeated them in
her mind. *I didn't think I needed help from anyone.
I guess I did.*

Mrs. Marshall looked up and watched Alex
closely. "You got through to her, Alex," she said
quietly. "That's what teaching is all about. Finding
a way to help someone discover her own abilities
and giving her the tools she needs to become all
she can."

"So, it's a little like that fishing story, right?"

"Something like that," Mrs. Marshall laughed.

"And it's what you and Mrs. Anderson have
been doing for me, isn't it?"

Mrs. Marshall smiled. "It's what you did for
Ronna. Now get a good night's sleep and I hope

I'll see you tomorrow after school. I've informed the team that I will annouce the alternate team member at the competition. I trust you will make the right choice for you and the team."

"I understand."

Walking down the empty hallway, she wondered why Mrs. Marshall and Mrs. Anderson took time with her. Once she got outdoors, she was hit with a cold blast of air that helped clear her head. The walk home was long and gloomy. She passed by the pet store and took note of the empty window. She would start work soon. At least that was something to look forward to, but it made her feel sad now that Miss Kitty was gone. When she arrived home, Alex went straight to her room, dropped her backpack on the floor, kicked her shoes off and flopped on her bed. She could see the corner of the blue construction paper peeking out of her bag and rolled over to pull it out. She read the words over again and repeated them out loud, *I didn't think I needed help from anyone. I guess I did.*

It hit her in a flash. That little girl was smarter that she knew. She pulled out her MATHCOUNTS t-shirt, held it up to admire it and said with renewed enthusiasm, "Ronna, you are right! There's nothing wrong with getting a little help."

24

The morning announcements were barely audible over the chatter in homeroom.

"Quiet, please," Mrs. Anderson instructed, just as the principal announced the afternoon's MATHCOUNTS Competition

> *West Middle School is proud to host five area teams at this year's MATHCOUNTS Chapter Competition which will begin at 4:30 in the auditorium. Please come out and support West. Good luck!*

The three chimes rang out to signal the end of the morning announcements.

Alex felt nervous about her decision to participate. The rest of the day seemed to drag and she could hardly eat her lunch. When she arrived to math class, Emily glanced at her, immediately turned her attention back to the group she was with and laughed loudly. Mrs. Marshall walked in, and the students settled in their seats.

"I hope to see you at the competition," she said quietly to Alex.

Alex took her seat without responding, though

her thoughts were racing. She couldn't wait for the bell to signal the end of the day. When it finally rang, she went to her locker, grabbed her t-shirt and made her way to the auditorium. The stage lights were on and it was being set for the competition. Emily was "holding court," strategizing with Janella and David. Not a hair was out of place, from her manicured fingernails to her neatly pressed shirt. Alex looked down at her crumpled t-shirt, jeans and sneakers.

I don't fit in. No one wants me to be here. She turned and ran down the hall, burst through the school doors and continued running all the way home. When she pushed open the front door she was startled to run into Danielle.

"What are you doing here?"

"I live here," Danielle replied.

"Why aren't you at work?"

"You are looking at a career woman, missy."

"Oh really, since when has cleaning become big business?"

"Not cleaning. I start work at Bella Salon tomorrow."

"Since when are you working at a salon?"

"Since tomorrow. Remember that salon Mom and I clean – the one with the nice brochure? They had a sign posted for a shampoo person, and I got the job. I picked up an information packet today to study. I talked to my advisor at school, and she said I can take classes to become a stylist during my senior year, so by the time I graduate I can get a pretty good job."

"Wow, you can do that? That's incredible," Alex said.

"I know!"

"That's what you said you were going to do, and now you are really going to do it!"

"I know," Danielle agreed again and grinned while observing her sister. "What's with the goofy t-shirt, and why do you look like you've been crying?"

"It's a long story."

"Try me, but give me the short version."

"I made the math team, I tried to do everything myself. I made us lose – twice – and we're competing against five schools. Everyone hates me. I don't fit in. I'm not pretty. Emily's horrible. Matt thinks she's perfect."

"Whoa, girl! Let's take this a little slower. You made the math team?"

"Yeah, I know, I'm a dork."

"No, that's really fantastic."

"It is?"

"Of course! Now how did you make everyone lose?"

"I kept answering the questions before I

113

checked with the team."

"Why doesn't that surprise me?"

"Thanks. That's why they hate me."

"I'm sure they don't hate you."

"They do."

"And who is Emily?"

"She's this incredibly smart girl, and everyone thinks she is wonderful, except she's not, she's really mean. She doesn't want me to be part of the team."

"She's jealous."

"I doubt it."

"And this Matt guy likes her?"

"Well, yeah. I really don't know why. But I don't really care."

"That's it?"

"That's it."

"So when is the big competition?"

"Four-thirty."

"Four-thirty on what day?"

"Um, today."

"Today?"

"Yes."

"What are you doing here, then?"

"I quit."

"What in the world did you quit for?"

"I don't know. I think I sorta made a mistake. Mrs. Marshall said I should stay."

"Uh, yeah, you made a mistake. You have to compete!"

"I do?"

"Of course you do, now let's get busy."

"Busy doing what?"

"You can't exactly go to the competition looking like that, now can you?" Danielle glanced at her watch. "We have less than an hour to whip you into shape. Let's see…"

"It's impossible."

"Honey, you ain't seen nothin' yet," Danielle said as she grabbed the telephone. "They don't call me Scissorhands Martinez for nothing!"

"Nobody calls you Scissorhands Martinez."

"Well they should!" Danielle was energized. "Meet me in our room in two minutes. Turn on the iron, plug in the flat iron, and I'll call a taxi in the meantime to come pick us up at 4:15."

"Us?"

"Are you kidding? I'm not going to miss this. My little sis is a brainiac."

Alex grinned at her sister. "We're going to ride in a taxi?"

"How else do you think we're going to get there on time?"

This is cool, Alex thought.

"Snap to it!" Danielle barked with a quick double clap of her hands.

Alex jumped to attention and ran upstairs with a sudden burst of energy. She was already ironing her competition shirt when Danielle joined her in their room.

"Good, slip your shirt on and come sit on the edge of the bed," Danielle directed. She took a wide-toothed comb and attempted to run it through the tangled mass of Alex's hair.

"Ouch!" Alex squirmed.

"Sorry, have you *ever* combed your hair?"

Danielle arranged her sister's hair with large claw-like clips so she could smooth each section one at a time. Next she grabbed a case from her dresser, placed it on the bed and opened it to reveal an assortment of cosmetics.

"Now remember, at your age, you don't need make-up, but for a special occasion, a little bit can go a long way. And plucking a few of those stray eyebrow hairs wouldn't hurt, either." She prompted her sister to look up, look down, close her eyes and pucker her lips while she deftly plucked and applied the make-up. She picked up a pair of scissors and snipped the edges of Alex's hair.

"Oh boy," Alex fussed as hair fell to the floor.

"Stop squirming!"

A horn sounded outside.

"Finished!" Danielle announced. The

116

transformation was complete. "Just in time!"

Alex jumped to her feet, grabbed her hoodie and headed for the door.

"Wait!" Danielle called. "Aren't you going to look in the mirror?"

Alex hesitated, then walked over to the mirror. She felt a strange sensation seeing the pretty reflection looking back at her. Her hair was sleek and styled, her eyes were lively, and the touch of gloss shining on her lips made her feel so feminine. She looked at her sister, and trying to mask her enthusiasm, fumbled for something to say.

"I know, I know, you're beautiful and you're welcome, now let's get going," Danielle commanded. "Too bad it's a math competition and not a beauty contest. I am good!"

"Very funny," Alex replied. Her heart was racing as she ran down the stairs. It was a quarter past four. The girls climbed into the back seat of the cab and looked out the windows as they were whisked to the school. As they passed the pet store, Danielle said, "Hey, aren't you supposed to be working?"

"Uh, not exactly," Alex slouched in her seat.

"You've got some explaining to do."

"I probably do. Look!" She quickly changed the subject. "Here we are, gotta run!" Alex undid her seatbelt and quickly left the car as Danielle paid the driver with a handful of crinkled one-dollar bills. Alex turned back and yelled, "Thanks!" as she ran to the entrance of the school.

~ ~ ~

Everyone was seated when Alex arrived at the auditorium. Winded from running down the hall, she guessed there were at least 400 people in the audience. Banners representing each of the six teams were displayed throughout the room. *Wow, this is a big deal,* she thought. She searched for Mrs. Marshall and spotted her standing in front at the end of the right aisle. As Alex walked toward her, Mrs. Marshall nodded and smiled, motioning for her to come forward.

The announcer was just finishing the introduction of the team from East, which was met with applause from the rival fans.

"Now, I'm pleased to introduce the team from West Middle School." The West students and families applauded as Emily, David and Janella were introduced. Mrs. Marshall handed the announcer a folded note that named the final team member for West, and he added, "and the fourth member of the West team is Alexandra Martinez."

Emily's smile melted into an expression of confusion, then one of disbelief as she saw Alex approach. Alex walked the rest of the way down the aisle with all eyes upon her. Her eyes were focused on her feet as she made her way tentatively toward the stage.

"Hit a home run!" she heard coming from the audience. She looked up to see Ronna kneeling in her seat wearing her favorite Cubs jersey. Ronna gave her a thumbs-up, and Alex responded with a wink. She took a deep breath, held her head up and briskly walked the rest of the way to join her team.

"You look fantastic!" Janella exclaimed.

"Wow!" is all David could say, while Emily stared with her jaw open.

"Teams, prepare to begin," and the first round commenced.

~ ~ ~

Mrs. Martinez arrived home early again that afternoon. She placed her keys in a little bowl near the door and turned on the lamp.

"Hello, is anyone home?" she called out. "Hello!" She figured Danielle must be out with her friends and then remembered Alex was at her new job. She decided to drop by Mr. Fillion's pet shop and surprise her. A short walk later, she arrived at the shop where Mr. Fillion was helping a customer at the cash register. Mrs. Martinez looked around for Alex while she waited, but did not see her.

"Mrs. Martinez," Mr. Fillion welcomed her. "What brings you here today?"

She smiled but was confused by his greeting. "Hello, Joseph. I'm here to see how Alexandra is doing. Thank you so much for the opportunity."

"I'm not sure if there's been a misunderstanding, but Alexandra isn't starting work until tomorrow," Mr. Fillion informed her. "She said she had to stay after school for a few days."

"She did?" Mrs. Martinez said with surprise.

"Yes, I'm sorry. Is there anything I can do to help?"

"Oh no, it's alright," she assured him. "It was good to see you." Her feeling of confusion began to change to anger as she quickened her pace to the school. *How could she lie to me about detention? She promised there'd be no more.* Mrs. Martinez marched straight to Mrs. Marshall's classroom, but when she arrived, she found only one boy in the room. Earl had come to retrieve a battery for Mrs. Marshall's camera.

"Hello," Mrs. Martinez said, "Do you know where Mrs. Marshall is?"

"Yes," Earl responded politely. "She's at the MATHCOUNTS Competition in the auditorium. I'm headed over there if you want me to show you the way."

"Yes, thank you," she said while they walked

together.

"I'm Earl," he said.

"I'm Mrs. Martinez."

"Oh," Earl nodded, "You're Alex's mom. Everyone was surprised to see her today. I was glad she came back. I guess you're pretty proud, huh?"

Mrs. Martinez tried to absorb what he was saying, but it made no sense to her at all. Earl held the door to the auditorium open for her and she quietly made her way in. She scanned the audience for her daughter, but couldn't locate her. She saw Mrs. Marshall in the front, but still no Alex.

"West?" the announcer called out.

"42 cents," a voice responded.

Mrs. Martinez recognized her daughter's voice and looked toward the stage. She studied the row of competitors from left to right but did not see Alex. Suddenly she backtracked to the left and realized it was Alex sitting with the West team members. She was striking and confident, the transformation was amazing. She slipped into a seat to watch.

"As we move into the Team Countdown Round, East leads by two points," the announcer said, and then introduced the first team problem.

The teams huddled together and Emily took the

lead. "Let's get busy, and remember, we work as a team." She glared at Alex, who took the demand as a challenge. Quickly consulting her calculator, Alex slammed her hand down on the bell.

The announcer called on her. "A six percent increase," she declared the answer confidently.

"That is incorrect." The audience groaned. Emily threw down her pencil in disgust. The team from East answered correctly and scored a point. Alex felt like a deer caught in the headlights. She looked at the sea of faces in the audience and saw Ronna. Their eyes locked for a moment, then Ronna abruptly looked down.

Alex could feel the sting of tears and took a deep breath, trying not to show emotion. *C'mon,* she thought to herself, *don't goof this up. For once, let someone help.* She saw Mrs. Marshall, who nodded to her with encouragement. Alex nodded back, took a deep breath and listened intently as the announcer offered the next question. As soon as it was delivered, the students got busy. Alex finished first and reached for the bell. Her three teammates stopped and watched her hand hover over it. It took all her might to restrain herself from ringing the bell, but she quickly withdrew her hand and said, "I got 16 cartons as the answer. What did you get?"

The three others agreed with her answer, and

Emily jumped up and smacked the bell. "16 cartons," she responded when the announcer called on her.

"Correct," the announcer proclaimed.

The next two questions followed a similar pattern. With each correct response, the West fans became more enthusiastic and stood at their seats as the team slapped high fives. The teams from East and West were clearly in the lead, and the match would be decided by the final question. Seconds after the announcer posed the question, the teams scrambled to arrive at the answer. A tense silence filled the room as the audience awaited the sound of the bell. Emily finished first and whispered her answer to the group. "The answer is 8."

"Yep, that's what I got," David agreed.

"I'm not sure. I don't really understand the problem," said Janella. "Alex, what did you get?"

"The answer is 12," Alex reported convincingly.

"Oh no!" David worried. "I think it's 8. Quick, we have to beat East to the bell."

Emily hastily rang the bell a split second before a team member from East did the same. The room fell silent and all eyes were on her. The correct answer would determine the winner of the competition.

"West, may we have your answer?" the announcer asked. Emily faltered for a moment and looked at her teammates.

"West?" the announcer encouraged.

"Alex, you say the answer," Emily said.

Caught off guard, Alex stiffened and looked at Emily in disbelief. Her heart pounded in her chest and her eyes darted from face to face in the audience. She spotted Matt and Mrs. Marshall, then Ronna who was sitting up on the edge of her seat. *Sometimes you just have to ask for help.* The words from Ronna's note raced through her mind. She inhaled deeply and let the air out slowly. "The answer is 8," she said confidently.

Emily held her breath while Janella and David held hands as if to give each other courage while they waited to learn the verdict.

"That is correct," the announcer said. "West is the Chapter Champion, winning by one point. Congratulations to all of today's teams for a very close match." The West competition team members jumped to their feet with shouts of delight, and the rest of the team rushed to the stage with whoops and hollers, embracing each other while the audience gave the teams a standing ovation.

Alex felt a flush of excitement as she connected with her teammates. Mrs. Marshall signaled her team to acknowledge the other teams who somberly were preparing to leave. The students shook each other's hands and remained on the stage to receive awards. Each West team member was given a small trophy. Mrs. Marshall instructed the students to meet in her classroom after visiting with friends and family who were in attendance. Alex made her way down the steps from the stage just as Ronna rushed toward her and gave her a bear hug.

"Hey, kid," Alex said with a grin.

"That was a homerun for sure!" Ronna exclaimed.

"Congratulations," Ronna's mother added. "Good luck at states."

States, Alex thought, *that's right, they would travel to the State Competition next!*

"So I'll see you after school for tutoring tomorrow?" Ronna asked.

"I don't think so, you have a real teacher starting this week," Alex replied.

"What do you mean? You're a real teacher!" Ronna corrected.

"Nah," Alex laughed sheepishly.

"You're right, Ronna. She's a very good teacher," Mrs. Marshall said, joining the girls.

"The best!" Ronna exclaimed.

Alex pulled Ronna's baseball cap over her eyes

and said, "See ya around, kid…I'll stop in and visit you."

"Okay, bye," Ronna turned to leave.

"Hey, Ronna," Alex called after her. "Would you do me a favor?"

"Sure, what?"

"Can you take care of this for me?" Alex held out her trophy for Ronna to take.

"Really?"

"Yeah. When you look at it, I want you to remember to study your math!"

"Gee, thanks!" Ronna took it carefully from Alex's hand, and ran to catch up with her mom, yelling, "Mom, I got a trophy, look!"

"So, how does it feel to be a teacher, Alex?" Mrs. Marshall asked.

"Pretty good. A little scary. But pretty good. I don't know how you do it. I could hardly handle one kid."

"We teachers get a little more practice than you had."

"I just wanted to say thank you, and I'm sorry," Alex said after a long pause.

"Sorry for what?"

"I just didn't get it. I didn't want to admit I needed help. I thought I could do everything myself."

"We all need a little help now and then. And

I think you'd be surprised to learn how many people are here to help and support you." She nodded toward Mrs. Anderson, who waved back enthusiastically and mouthed, *Congratulations.*

"I'm starting to believe that. But I feel bad 'cause you both spent so much of your time on me."

"It's time well spent, Alex. Every student has so much to offer. It's my job to help him or her discover it and then make the most of it."

"And, um, one more thing. I have a confession."

"What's that?" Mrs. Marshall asked curiously.

"I really like math."

Mrs. Marshall laughed, "I know you do, and you are good at it, too!"

"I just thought everyone would think I was a geek."

"And was that the case?"

"I don't know, but I realized it doesn't matter what everyone else thinks. I think it's pretty cool."

"Good for you. I'll see you back in my room in a few minutes for a group photo and some details about the State Competition. And remember, tomorrow we will all be wearing our t-shirts to school."

"Well, I don't know if I'd go that far!" Alex

teased.

Mrs. Marshall smiled at her response, gave her a hug and whispered, "Now I think there is someone else here who supports you more than you know." She moved aside to reveal Mrs. Martinez standing by herself about ten feet away.

"Mom!" Alex said with surprise and walked toward her. "What...Why are...How did you know?"

"I went to visit you at your new job, but you were not there."

"Oh," Alex's face fell. "Sorry."

"Alexandra, why would you not tell me about this?"

"I thought you...everyone would think I was silly to believe that I could be smart, and I thought why should I bother if I'm not going to college? And everyone was making fun of Matt when he was on the team, and I'm already different, I didn't want everyone making fun of me."

"You are right, you are different, but that's what makes you so very special. You are smart and strong, and you can do whatever you put your mind to. You proved that today. I'm very proud of you."

"You aren't mad?"

"You should not have lied to me about going to work, but I'm not mad, just very proud."

"I guess I am too, kid." Danielle joined the two and tapped her sister on the head like patting a dog. Alex poked her back, causing a quick exchange of pokes and giggles.

"Okay, girls, let's not ruin this lovely moment. Besides, I have news to share, too." The girls stopped their horseplay to listen to their mother.

"The delicatessen I clean is not renewing their lease and closed their doors for good today. And, I think I've had enough of the cleaning business."

"Gee, Mom, sorry to hear you are losing a client," Danielle said with concern. "Do you need help finding another one? And if you're tired, Alex and I can help you out to give you a break."

Alex cringed at the thought and Danielle nudged her from behind. "Sure, Mom, we can help out," she agreed half-heartedly.

"No, thank you girls, that won't be necessary," Mrs. Martinez smiled. "It's not that I wouldn't enjoy working with you, but it's time that you two start following your own dreams…and for me to follow mine."

"What do you mean?" Danielle asked.

"That little deli is in just the right spot and just the right size to open the Martinez Grill, serving the best Hispanic food in town!" she announced.

"Mom! That's wonderful!" Alex exclaimed.

"Wow! I'm so happy for you," Danielle hugged

her. "It's what you and Dad always talked about. He would be so proud."

"I know," Mrs. Martinez teared up. "Today he would be proud of all of us. So, it looks like we will be the three working women now."

"To the working women!" Danielle raised an imaginary glass and they all repeated together, "To the working women!"

"Perhaps we will stop at Mr. Fillion's pet shop on the way home to explain today's confusion," Mrs. Martinez raised her eyebrow at Alex.

"Right." Alex cringed. "Sorry I didn't exactly tell the truth about that. I really can't wait to start."

The three headed toward the back of the auditorium and Alex flushed when she saw Matt standing at the doorway. Mrs. Martinez saw Matt smile at Alex and said, "Why don't you catch up with your sister and me at the main door?" Danielle lagged behind with her sister, and Mrs. Martinez continued, "And Danielle wants to come with me, right, Danielle?"

"Oh, yes, I want to go with Mom," Danielle repeated sarcastically and reluctantly joined her mother, but not before silently forming the words, *Alex likes Matt!*

Alex rolled her eyes and said, "Why don't you two go ahead without me? I'll walk home later because I still have to go to Mrs. Marshall's class."

"Okay, sis," Danielle said slyly and gave her sister an exaggerated wink.

Alex composed herself and approached Matt.

"Hey."

"Hey," he greeted her. "Good job."

"Thanks."

They stood in a moment of awkward silence.

"Well, I guess I should go," Alex said. "They are waiting for us in Mrs. Marshall's room."

"Oh, sure, right." Matt fumbled for words. "I thought you changed," he finally said.

"No, it's just my hair."

"No, that's not what I meant. I mean, it was really cool how you were behind me when I got on the math team when everyone else thought I was nuts. But you changed when you got on the team. It's like you had to prove something to everyone else."

"I guess I thought I did. But it turned out that I really only needed to prove something to myself."

"Did you?"

"It took an eight-year-old to knock some sense into me, but I think I'm starting to get the idea."

"I'm glad the old Alex is back."

"That's the new *improved* Alex!"

"Yeah, the hair *is* kinda nice."

"Alex," Emily interrupted. "Hi, Matt," she paused to smile at him.

"Hey, Emily, way to go!" Matt replied. Alex cringed.

Emily turned off her charm and turned her attention back to Alex. "Mrs. Marshall wants us in her room now," she commanded and walked off to the classroom.

"You two should try to get along. She's not that bad."

"I gotta go," Alex said while thinking, *that will be the day.*

"See ya."

"See ya," Alex replied over her shoulder as she hurried to Mrs. Marshall's room.

The students assembled for a photo and Mrs. Marshall praised their work. "Nothing like a close call!" she said. "I'd say we've all accomplished a lot over the past months. Not only did you do an excellent job with your math problems, you learned to work together as a team. I'm proud of each of you. Now I expect to see everyone Thursday after school to start practicing for the State Competition. I was just informed that the National Competition will be in New York City this year, so let's work hard, because I sure would like to see Broadway!"

New York City! Alex thought and smiled to herself. *Now that was something to work for. That would be a dream come true.* She wandered out the door to the hallway.

"Alex," Emily called after her.

Now what? Alex wondered.

"You forgot to pick up your certificate," Emily said and handed her an attractive certificate of participation that each member was given.

"Thanks."

"You're welcome." The two stood face-to-face in silence, then simultaneously blurted out, "I'm sorry," then, "No, I'm sorry," and erupted in nervous laughter.

"You did a really good job today," Emily offered.

"Thanks. You did, too. Why did you let me give the final answer?"

"Why did you give my answer and not your own?"

"Seemed like the right thing to do."

"Yeah, me too."

"We're pretty different," Alex observed.

"We're really different, aren't we?" Emily agreed.

"You do a good job keeping everyone organized. That's not my strong suit," Alex pointed out.

"I wish I could be as easy-going as you. I'm so

tightly wound, my parents are always after me to do more and better," Emily added.

"Are you kidding? I was a nervous wreck! I can't really imagine anyone doing better than you do in school."

"Thanks! I'm so excited about going to the State Competition, we are going to have to practice really hard." Emily paused, then added, "Maybe we should get together at my house to practice sometime."

"Really?" Alex responded with surprise. "Sure! Can you imagine if we actually went to the National Competition? My dream is to see New York City."

"Mine, too!" Emily exclaimed, "The shopping!" at the same time Alex said, "The museums!"

"Okay, we will do both," Emily laughed. "But we will need new outfits. By the way, I love what you did with your hair."

"My sister did it for me."

"Wow! She's really good. I wish I could wear my hair that way."

"I'm sure she would be glad to do your hair, she loves it. She's going to be a stylist," Alex pointed out.

"That would be terrific."

"Hey, Emily, are you ready to go?" Matt called out from the end of the hallway. "My mom is here to pick us up."

"Be there in a minute," Emily called back.

Alex sighed, "He's so nice." She felt a little pang of jealousy.

"I guess so. He's a little nuts," Emily said.

"You're really lucky."

"Lucky? What do you mean?"

"It's obvious Matt likes you, and, well, I thought you liked him," Alex said, puzzled by Emily's indifference.

"Sure I do, but he's my cousin, so I sorta have to like him."

"He's your cousin?" Alex asked in disbelief.

"Yep, and I gotta go 'cause my aunt is driving us home. I'll see you tomorrow!"

"Okay, see ya," Alex said, still stunned. She grinned and her cheeks flushed. *Cousins?* She watched Emily walk down the hall. It was hard to believe she actually looked forward to spending time with her. *Emily must have really changed and come to her senses,* she thought. *Or maybe I have.* As the janitor headed her way with a wide mop, she realized she was the only one left in the hall and headed for the main door.

Alex's walk home passed quickly with her head filled with the afternoon's events. As she came up to the pet shop she felt energized. She would start work this week and earn her own money. She loved the feeling of growing up and becoming responsible.

Mr. Fillion greeted her and reviewed her duties. She explained why her mother was confused about why she wasn't working that day, and he was very understanding. Alex decided he wasn't so mean after all and would be a fine boss. He congratulated her on the team's win, and she said goodbye. On the way out she spotted a tail sliding back and forth from under the fish food display. She knelt down to investigate and discovered a small cat swiping at a bug that was trying to make a getaway.

"Miss Kitty!" she exclaimed. Alex shimmied the cat out from under the display and held the little ball of fur close, her heart filled with joy. "She's here, you didn't sell her?" Alex checked with Mr. Fillion, worried that her discovery was too good to be true.

"That's correct," he confirmed. "The reason that she was no longer for sale is that she is now the shop cat, and I expect that you will take good care of her here."

"You bet I will!" Alex agreed with glee. Miss Kitty meowed and squirmed out of her arms, hot on the trail of the bug again. Alex walked the rest of the way home brimming with happiness.

A few minutes later she arrived and was

welcomed by a makeshift sign that read "CONGRATULATIONS." Danielle had stapled 15 sheets of notebook paper together, each with a letter drawn on it in colored marker, and carefully tacked it up to drape above the doorway. She entered and received hugs from her sister and mother.

"Come, let's celebrate, Alexandra," her mother said cheerfully as she led them into the kitchen. "I'm baking cookies!"

"Sounds great, but I have something I have to do. It will only take a minute and I'll be right down." Alex ran up to the girls' room, shut the door and collapsed backwards onto her bed with her arms stretched out. She let out a little screech of delight.

"Is everything okay up there?" her mother called.

"Everything is absolutely wonderful, Mom." Alex yelled back.

She stared at the ceiling thinking about how her life had changed for the better in such a short time. *What if I never took a chance? What if I never asked for help?* She thought about how Mrs. Marshall and Mrs. Anderson had helped her and the unexpected satisfaction she got from teaching Ronna. She thought about how much fun it was being part of a team, and the new friends she was making. Just a week ago, she would never have thought she would ever see eye-to-eye with Emily. She looked forward to seeing Matt and the old gang at lunch tomorrow. Ben and Brian could make fun of her if they wanted to, but she would wear her team shirt. Nothing could take away the pride of winning and the excitement she felt about going to the State Competition. *What if they could go to the National Competition in New York City?*

"New York City!" Alex exclaimed, and sliding off the bed, got on her knees to search under it. She pulled out some books, slippers, a box and finally a rolled-up poster. She carefully smoothed it out and admired it. "I guess anything is possible," she said with conviction, and tacked it back up on her wall. Alex stood back and addressed her poster, "New York City, look out 'cause here I come!" She gave it a wink and turned to run downstairs to celebrate.

25

The next morning, Mrs. Marshall entered her classroom tired from the previous day's events. A small envelope with her name on it lay waiting on the desk. She carefully opened it and read:

Dear Mrs. Marshall,

I thought teaching was just about textbooks. You showed me differently, and I thank you for that. I don't know exactly what I'll be when I grow up, but you taught me I can be anything I want, even a teacher. I think I could be a good one, like you. It's harder than I thought, but it really makes you feel good when you get through to a kid like Ronna. . .or me.

You said that you had a special teacher in your life who helped you find your way. You will always be that special teacher to me.

Your student,
Alex

THE END

**Meet
Stephanie Pace Marshall, Ph.D.**

**Educator, Founding President,
CEO, and President Emerita,
Illinois Mathematics and
Science Academy**

*"Mind shaping is
world shaping"*

Born in the Bronx, New York, Stephanie Pace Marshall says she grew up in the world's most diverse and dynamic cultural and scientific playground. "In a very real sense, New York City was my classroom and learning laboratory," she explains. She and her family loved spending weekends at the Bronx Zoo and all the other amazing places that make the city an exhilarating and stimulating place for a child to explore...the Metropolitan Museum, the Hayden Planetarium, the Joffrey Ballet, the Museum of Natural History, the Metropolitan Opera, Radio City Music Hall and much more. "It was a rich kaleidoscopic playground of ideas and possibilities, and as a child, I was interested in everything!

"Learning was joyful to me. I grew up immersed in science, mathematics, music and the performing and visual arts. My father was a nuclear mechanical engineer, and before my mother became a teacher of autistic children she was a professional singer. Music and dance are still very important to me."

A curious and very committed student, Dr. Marshall originally intended to pursue medicine and theology – she wanted to be a surgeon and a minister, but she says what she actually wanted to become in third grade is exactly who she is now!

"I was a serious student, and when the teacher asked our third grade class what each of us wanted to be when we grew up, I said I wanted to be a lion. All the kids laughed, but my teacher didn't think it was funny and scheduled a meeting with my mother. What my mother said was one of her greatest gifts to me. She put her arm around my shoulder and said, 'Stephanie, the only reason the other children don't want to become a lion is because they don't have the courage!' Although, of course, I didn't want to become a real lion, I realize now that this metaphor is a significant grounding for me. My work now is to use my voice to tell the story of possibilities for all of our children."

That work is to design conditions that will likely ignite and nurture the intellectual and creative potentials of children. Her personal commitment is to "do everything I can to create conditions that liberate the goodness and genius of all children for the world."

According to Dr. Marshall, "Mind shaping is world shaping. Education is the most important work of any culture because the minds that teachers help develop will shape our future and our world. How we think, come to know and make sense of our world is how we choose to live. It is who we become. And how we live is how the world is shaped. This idea is the driving force for everything I do."

Teachers have astonishing influence on developing the hearts, minds and spirits of children, all of whom will help to create our future.

"When you are teaching a child, you have no idea who you may be influencing. Whenever I talk to a child, I honor and encourage them just as I would if I knew he or she would grow up to become Mother Teresa, Albert Einstein, Rosa Parks or Neil Armstrong."

A teacher with experience at every educational level, from elementary through graduate school, Dr. Marshall is internationally recognized as a pioneer and innovative leader, teacher, speaker and writer on issues of leadership, transformative learning and schooling, gifted and talented education, and mathematics and science education. She is the founding and former President of the Illinois Mathematics and Science Academy (IMSA), Aurora, Illinois.

Prior to becoming IMSA's founding President, Dr. Marshall served as the Superintendent of Schools in Batavia, Illinois. She was named superintendent in 1984 when there was only one other K - 12 female school superintendent in Illinois in more than 900 school districts. She also has worked as a national strategic planner and served as a member of the graduate faculties at National Louis University and Loyola University. She has served as President of the Association for Supervision and Curriculum Development (the world's largest professional educational association), an advisor to the Education Task Force of the President's Council of Science Advisors, and as a member of the National Academy of Sciences Committee on Advanced Study in Mathematics and Science in U.S. High Schools.

Dr. Marshall was selected by the RJR Nabisco Corporation as one of the nation's most innovative educational leaders and was chosen twice by *Executive Educator* magazine and the National School Boards Association as one of North America's 100 Top School Executives.

The *Chicago Sun Times* selected her as one of the ten most powerful women in education and one of the 100 most powerful women in Chicago; she has received numerous awards and recognitions for her distinctive leadership. In 2005, she was inducted into the Lincoln Academy of Illinois and received the Order of Lincoln, the state's highest award for achievement that advances humanity. It is among her most prized awards because, she says, "As an educator, my life and my work have always been dedicated to advancing the human condition."

A member of many local, national and international organizations, she also serves as an international consultant, keynote speaker and writer on issues critical to educational transformation. She has written more than 35 articles, and her book, *The Power to Transform: Leadership that Brings Learning and Schooling to Life*, won the 2007 Educator's Award from Delta Kappa Gamma.

Dr. Marshall received a B.A. from Queens College in New York City, an M.A. degree in Curriculum Philosophy from the University of Chicago, and a Ph.D. in Educational Administration and Industrial Relations from Loyola University of Chicago. She holds four Honorary Doctorates from Illinois Wesleyan University, Aurora University, North Central College and Dominican University.

GIRLS WANT TO KNOW...

Know How®   ASKED DR. PACE MARSHALL:

WHO WERE YOUR ROLE MODELS?

My family, especially my parents, were my first and most lasting role models. From my father, I learned the value of the scientific mind and a precise way of understanding the world. From my mother, I learned the value of the artistic mind and kaleidoscopic ways of seeing the world. Together they helped me blend both ways of knowing, which has helped me become who I am.

There were other role models as I grew up. When I was ten, I remember reading the story, and actually seeing it unfold on television, of Rosa Parks [an African-American civil rights activist who in 1955 became famous when she refused to give up her seat on a bus to make room for a white passenger]. I said to myself that someday I would meet this woman so that I could thank her for her courageous action. Thirty years later, I had the opportunity to do so when, as President of the Illinois Mathematics and Science Academy, I invited her to speak with our students and more than 500 guests, so that we could not only hear her story, but thank her for her extraordinary commitment and courage in the fight against racial injustice.

Others whom I admire greatly include Jane Goodall [a noted humanitarian and environmentalist who is known for her scientific thinking and revolutionary studies of chimpanzees], and a young boy named Craig Kielburger. I met Craig when he was 12. He had created an international foundation to help children through education. He continues his efforts to end child labor around the world and provide educational opportunities for all children.

WHAT ATTRIBUTES DO YOU ASSOCIATE WITH SUCCESS IN YOUR FIELD?

First and foremost, having success in one's field is being connected to colleagues who share your passion and vision for what might be possible. It is when we work together with "kindred spirits" that we can be the most successful. There are other attributes, of course, that I also connect with success. They are to learn deeply, have an insatiable curiosity, be open to the world, maintain a passion for learning including reading, exploring and visiting new places, and continue to deepen your own understanding.

You can't turn children on unless you are "turned on" yourself!

Teaching enables us to share with children our passion and our own desire to keep learning. You must know your discipline thoroughly. I have a very strong belief that there are very few limits to what we can become.

146

A truly successful educator is one who builds
the capacity of others to realize their dreams
and believes in children and their ability to do
astonishing things to change the world.

For instance, the incredible Bonnie St. John lost a leg when she was just five years old, but went on to win a silver medal skiing in the Paralympic Games. Teachers must let children know that they will be there for them and that they are supportive of their dreams.

WHAT ARE SOME EDUCATIONAL ROUTES TO BECOMING A TEACHER?

The typical routes to becoming a teacher are to attend a community college and then a four-year college, or to begin in a four-year college where you are majoring in a content field and then studying to become a teacher. Teachers now also are pursuing Master's Degrees in their fields and many are seeking additional advanced degrees so they are continually prepared for the challenges of their careers. Usually after two or three years of college (although in some places it begins in the freshman year) students are engaged in student teaching. This is an opportunity for students to get into classrooms and to work with mentors and experienced teachers, and to find out if they really love working with children and helping them learn.

Because we don't always know what we want to be

when we're young, it is not uncommon for people in other fields such as engineering, science, mathematics, technology, business, marketing or law to decide after they have been in their career for several years that they really love teaching and want to become a teacher. Many states provide pathways for alternative teacher certification, so a professional who has already earned a B.A. or M.A. in his or her field does not have to go back to college for four years to earn a teaching degree.

ARE THERE OTHER JOBS THAT MIGHT PREPARE ONE FOR TEACHING?

As a child or teenager, if you think you might be interested in teaching, it's important to get involved with younger children as soon as you can. Babysitting, taking children on field trips, volunteering in park districts, working at YMCAs, teaching in Saturday or Sunday schools and participating in community service are all excellent opportunities for you to begin working with children to see if it's something you really want to do. You also can gain wonderful experience for teaching by working as a counselor, nurse or social worker in human services organizations.

Although you may not begin by wanting to be a teacher, there are other jobs in the social and human services, even in law and marketing, that can prepare you for the complexities and challenges of working with 25 or 30 highly curious minds.

WHAT ARE SOME UPPER LEVEL POSITIONS TO WHICH A TEACHER COULD ASPIRE?

Within the education field, a teacher can move into administration, become a department chairperson, a principal, a dean, college president or a state superintendent of education. Or one can even prepare to move into policy and work in many state, national and international educational agencies…even aspire to become the United States Secretary of Education!

Teaching is a field with skills that are transferable, and they can take you anywhere and everywhere! For instance, a teacher who knows how to "manage a classroom" can become an entrepreneur and manage his or her own business, or manage and lead a division of a company or become its CEO. Success in teaching requires an exceptional understanding of relationships and the capacity to motivate people to do their best and realize their potentials. These are tremendous skills that will make teachers exemplary staff members in any profession.

WHAT DO YOU LIKE MOST ABOUT YOUR JOB?

As a teacher and leader, the most joyful thing for me is having the chance to ignite the talents of others. When I help people see their own amazing gifts and talents, and use them in ways that astonish even them, I have an enormous sense of accomplishment. "Seeing light bulbs turn on" is one of the greatest joys of teaching.

WHAT IS THE MOST CHALLENGING ASPECT OF TEACHING?

The most challenging aspect of teaching is to know each child so well that you know the conditions that you must create to ignite and nurture his or her own goodness and genius.

WHAT IS THE MOST IMPORTANT THING YOU HAVE LEARNED THROUGH WORKING?

Be grateful and generous. Understand that we each have special gifts, and no one can make your unique contribution but you. Don't apologize for your dreams, follow your heart, be bold. Carl Sagan said, "Dreams are maps." Slow down so you can learn things well. Honor and celebrate life, and be gentle with the earth. Be stewards of your gifts, passions and dreams. Say "yes" to belonging, because we are all connected in some way. Find your own voice, speak your truth. Decide what you want your name on. Our names are our integrity, and matter more than anything.

WERE YOU EVER INSPIRED BY A TEACHER?

My most vivid memory of being inspired by a teacher happened when I was taking my final exam in my eighth grade physics class. In an instant and with a single gesture, my teacher taught me how to believe in and trust myself. The exam consisted of just one question: Given the distance between the earth and sun, how long would it take an explosion on the sun to be heard on the earth? I read the question several times and said to myself, "That's a silly question. We wouldn't hear it." However, I looked around and saw

150

all my classmates busily working on the question, using their calculators to determine the answer. And I kept thinking, "But you wouldn't hear the explosion." So I went up to my teacher and said, "Miss Dynes, you wouldn't hear the explosion." She looked at me, put her finger to her lips as if to quiet me, and then she winked! I went back to my seat and wrote, "We would not hear it." This was a wonderful lesson in learning to not be distracted by the actions and voices of those around us, but to trust our own minds.

WHAT ADVICE WOULD YOU GIVE A YOUNGSTER WHO EXPRESSED INTEREST IN BECOMING A TEACHER?

First and foremost, discover what it is you are passionate about, develop your curiosity and seek opportunities to study and learn as much as you can. We tend to teach "who we are," and we find the most joy when we are teaching what it is that we love, so decide what it is you love, and then pursue that with great passion.

Spend time with younger children to see if you enjoy teaching them and creating conditions for them to experience their unknown possibilities. Do everything you can to see if this experience brings you joy and great satisfaction. Teaching is a very creative act and it requires relationships, a deep respect for children and a covenant with them to help them become all that they can be.

WHAT HOBBIES/PASSIONS DO YOU HAVE?

I collect kaleidoscopes, hundreds of them! I'm fascinated by their interconnections, magic, mystery, unpredictability, patterns and relationships. They are the perfect combination of art and science. I also love to write and read poetry. It is another language that can take us places. And when I get stuck writing, I dance!

OF WHICH ASPECTS OF YOUR CAREER AND PERSONAL LIFE ARE YOU MOST PROUD?

In relation to my personal life, I've been blessed with a wonderful and loving husband and supportive family and friends who encourage me to do what I love. Writing my first book and getting published has also been a great joy. And as the Founding President of the Illinois Mathematics and Science Academy, I had a remarkable opportunity to create something from scratch, which is very rare in my profession. Today it is internationally recognized as one of the finest institutions of its kind. I am proud of the remarkable students and people involved with IMSA who ensure that the organization's voice, vision and programs are available to more and more teachers and children around the world.

 AND

EXPLORING CAREERS
Make a Plan!
www.girlsknowhow.com

When I grow up, I would like to be a:

1._____

2._____

3._____

If I could have any job, I would be a _____

Describe why you would like this job (For instance: I like to
be active, I'm good at math or science, I like to read or write.
I like adventure, travel, helping people, it pays a lot.)

1._____

2._____

3._____

Whom do I know personally that has a job in this field?

_____

Is there anyone famous who has this type of job?

_____

153

What will I need to do this job well? (check all that apply)

____ Good grades

____ High school education

____ Some college or more school after high school

____ A special skill (what is it?)_____

____ Special training (what kind?)_____

____ Other_____

How can I learn more about this job?

___ Get a book from the library

___ Interview someone who has this job

___ Research this profession on the Internet
(with parents' permission)

___ Spend a day at work with someone who has this job

___ Look for what kind of jobs in this field are listed in the
newspaper employment section

I PLEDGE TO LEARN MORE ABOUT
CAREER OPPORTUNITIES

List what you will do to learn more about this job:

1. This week, I will_____

2. This month, I will_____

3. Next month, I will_____

Signed_____ Date_____